basic

PUNCTUATION

DON SHIACH

JOHN MURRAY

Other titles in the series:

Basic Grammar	Don Shiach	ISBN	0 7195 7028 X
Basic Spelling	Michael Temple	ISBN	0 7195 7026 3
Basic Written English	Don Shiach	ISBN	0 7195 7030 1

© Don Shiach 1995
First published 1995 by
John Murray (Publishers) Ltd, a member of the Hodder Headline Group
338 Euston Road,
London, NW1 3BH

Reprinted 1998, 1999, 2001, 2002, 2003, 2004, 2005

Layouts by Mick McCarthy
Illustration by Art Construction and David Farris
Typeset by Servis Filmsetting Ltd, Longsight,
Manchester.
Printed in Europe by the Alden Group, Oxford

A CIP record for this book is available from the
British Library.

ISBN 0 7195 7027 1

CONTENTS

INTRODUCTION

WHAT CAN THIS BOOK DO FOR ME?

Punctuation is the system that divides what we write into separate parts in order to make our meaning clearer. Without punctuation our writing would be a stream of words that would be almost impossible to understand.

SO I SAID TO HIM AND I DIDN'T MINCE MY WORDS WHAT DO YOU THINK YOU'RE DOING I WASN'T GOING TO PUT UP WITH THAT WAS I NO WAY CATCH ME NOT ON YOUR NELLY 'FRAID NOT SON...

So, the better we understand and use the rules of punctuation, the more able we are to express ourselves clearly and effectively. This helps us to make a good impression when it is important to do so – for example:

in an exam	filling in forms	making an application for a job
	writing letters	

- In these situations people who use punctuation correctly are at an advantage.
- If the way we communicate is not clear, then people may not make the effort to understand what we have written.
- Understanding punctuation rules and applying them to your writing of English can help you present yourself to the rest of the world.

In speech, there is a kind of in-built punctuation: when you are speaking to someone, you naturally pause or change your voice slightly between phrases or sentences. These pauses and changes help your listeners to make sense of what you are saying. If someone were to speak in a monotone and without pauses, this would not give listeners a chance to take in and understand what is being said, and it would be difficult for communication to take place.

In written communication of all kinds, marks of punctuation divide words into groups so that listeners can understand which words and phrases belong together. Without punctuation, written communication becomes a confusing string of words. Look at this example:

After intense pressure the home team scored in the second half much against the run of play the visitors managed to equalise through a goal by their star striker Rovers then went ahead however once again the score was levelled when a tragic mistake by the home centre-half led to an own goal late in the game the home team increased its pressure but several chances went begging the replay will be on Tuesday next starting at eight o'clock tickets will be on sale from tomorrow.

This report of a football match is without any punctuation marks. This makes it much more difficult to understand – the reader has to guess what the writer had in mind. Now consider how the placing of punctuation marks in the report can alter the meaning. In the two versions below, the changing of the punctuation alters important details in the report.

After intense pressure, the home team scored. In the second half, much against the run of play, the visitors managed to equalise through a goal by their star striker. Rovers then went ahead, however. Once again the score was levelled. When a tragic mistake by the home centre-half led to an own goal late in the game, the home team increased its pressure but several chances went begging. The replay will be on Tuesday next. Starting at eight o'clock, tickets will be on sale from tomorrow.

After intense pressure, the home team scored in the second half. Much against the run of play, the visitors managed to equalise. Through a goal by their star striker, Rovers then went ahead. However, once again the score was levelled when a tragic mistake by the home centre-half led to an own goal. Late in the game, the home team increased its pressure but several chances went begging. The replay will be on Tuesday next, starting at eight o'clock. Tickets will be on sale from tomorrow.

So remember the following key points:

- Punctuation marks help you make yourself completely clear to your reader.
- Ask yourself what it is you are trying to communicate and then use punctuation as an aid to writing it clearly.
- It often helps to read something aloud and check that the punctuation marks that you have used are correctly placed to convey the exact meaning you intended.
- Put yourself in the position of your reader and decide whether your use of punctuation has made the meaning clear.

HOW WILL THIS BOOK HELP ME?

This book will help you to identify and use correctly the different items of punctuation. These are:

- capital letters
- full stops
- commas
- speech marks (also called quotation marks or inverted commas)
- semi-colons
- colons
- brackets (also called parentheses)
- dashes
- hyphens
- apostrophes
- question marks
- exclamation marks

These can be thought of as language tools and if you know how to use them you will be better equipped to use the language.

You also need to know how to use these basic language tools in **sentences** and paragraphs. This book will help you to construct your writing by using sentences and paragraphs correctly and appropriately.

The first thing you should do is to use the **Self-assessment questionnaire** on page 4 to check your own strengths and weaknesses. Then you can concentrate on those areas where you need most practice.

PUTTING IT INTO PRACTICE

The aim of learning how to use punctuation is to be able to speak and write as expertly and clearly as possible. In this book, you will be given plenty of opportunities to check that you have understood and can use each kind of punctuation mark.

The **Checkpoints** allow you to make sure you have understood the purpose of the particular punctuation mark that has just been explained. The **Activities** then give you a chance to use the rules you have learnt. You can check that you are using punctuation marks appropriately by consulting the answers given at the back of the book.

Then it is up to you to practise applying what you have learned. Making the transfer between acquiring knowledge and putting it into practice is the crucial test for any new skill. Learning rules is pointless unless you are able to apply them. As you work your way through this book, make sure you look out for opportunities in everyday life to use what you have learnt in order to **write what you really mean**.

SELF-ASSESSMENT QUESTIONNAIRE

To test your present level of knowledge of punctuation, attempt the following exercises. Once you have completed the questionnaire, check the answers in the section at the back of this book and award yourself marks accordingly. Then check what the results tell you about your current knowledge of punctuation according to the marking key and assessment guide on page 6.

1 Read the following newspaper report which is totally lacking in punctuation. Rewrite the report inserting capital letters, commas, speech marks, apostrophes, question marks and full stops where you think they are necessary.

> sources close to the prime minister insist that he is not contemplating calling a general election recent problems facing the government had increased speculation that mr gray may decide to put his governments policies to the test by calling a snap election justin pockitt the chancellor of the exchequer also denied yesterday that an election was imminent
>
> we have had a few setbacks admitted mr pockitt the by-election results were particularly disappointing but our support in the country is still solid I believe that point of view was endorsed by violet cutter the health minister who said we were going to the country only a few political journalists its stuff and nonsense
>
> despite the official denials mps are standing by in case there is a sudden announcement theres a feeling in the air said one junior member with a slim majority all the statements in the world won't quell the election fever he added

2 The sentences in the article below have all been run together: there are no full stops or capital letters to indicate where one sentence ends and another begins. Rewrite the article with capital letters and full stops correctly inserted and add any other punctuation marks that have been omitted.

PARIS PUTS ON THE GLITTER

fashion shows this week in paris have brought back glitz and glamour to the catwalks the fashion folk of the french capital thronged to the latest shows of the leading parisian designers including jean-paul satie and yobbo streetwise the british couturier critics have gone wild over yobbos tibetan themes the twenty-one-year-old genius of the frock world said hed always been a fan of tibet and had wanted to incorporate tibetan styles into one of his collections asked why he no longer worked in britain streetwise claimed he had never really been appreciated in his own country i had to come to france to flower and mature yobbo stated as he was surrounded by hundreds of adoring fans i think its rather sad dont you the cheapest yobbo creation will set his fans back two thousand pounds thats not bad going for a kid from bermondsey crowed streetwise at the end of a hectic days selling still my frocks are worth every penny he added modestly

3 Read the following opening to a story. Part of the passage consists of direct speech (the actual words said by characters in the story); these sections, like the rest of the passage, have been left unpunctuated. Rewrite the passage, inserting speech marks, full stops, commas, capital letters, apostrophes, question and exclamation marks where you think necessary. In addition, divide the passage up into paragraphs where you think this is appropriate.

but where is the money going to come from jan asked youre full of great plans but what can we do to make it happen i have a scheme rod answered a scheme that cant fail you and your schemes jan exclaimed im tired of your schemes they inevitably fail as sure as god made little apples youre wrong this time said rod youre very wrong so what is this great scheme then were going to carry out a sting retorted rod a sting what are you talking about you know what a sting is said rod even you know that its an elaborate fiddle a con a trick a wheeze and illegal said jan of course its illegal all stings are illegal but well only be stealing money from people who deserve to lose it i see said jan so that makes it all right i suppose as long as these people were stealing from are not very nice that excuses the crime yes said rod thats just nonsense jan replied just an excuse for being a criminal wait till you hear about my plan i dont want to hear about it its very clever i told you i dont want to hear about it itll be fun too fun it wont be fun being in jail we wont go to jail because this sting is perfect no one will ever trace it to us famous last words said jan count me out youll change your mind once i explain it to you i wont yes you will

5

Assess what you know about punctuation by turning to the answers on page 81. Award yourself one mark for each correction you made then check your total against the scores given below.

Score between 330 and 344: you know your punctuation very well.
Score between 300 and 330: your knowledge of punctuation is quite strong, but you need to brush up on some points.
Score between 250 and 299: you definitely need to improve some aspects of your use of punctuation.
Score between 200 and 249: there are numerous weaknesses which you should correct.
Score between 150 and 199: you definitely need to work very hard at your use of punctuation.
Score between 100 and 149: you clearly have serious difficulty with punctuation.
Score below 100: you can only improve!

1
SENTENCES

TYPES OF SENTENCE

1 This bill is now due for payment.
2 Do you support experiments on animals?
3 Do not go beyond this point.
4 Elvis Is Brill!

Each of the above are sentences of one kind or another.
Sentence 1 makes a statement.
Sentence 2 asks a question.
Sentence 3 gives an instruction.
Sentence 4 is an exclamation.
The feature they all share, however, is that they make sense on their own.
They are **complete sentences**. They do not require any other words to
make complete sense. They make a statement, ask a question, give an
instruction or express an emotion.
Two other features they all share are to do with punctuation.

• All four start with a capital letter:
This bill. . .
Do you support. . .
Do not go. . .
Elvis. . .
• All four end with a punctuation mark:
. . . for payment. (full stop)
. . . on animals? (question mark)
. . . this point. (full stop)
. . . is brill! (exclamation mark)

A sentence starts with a capital letter to indicate where it begins.
A sentence ends with a punctuation mark (a full stop, a question or
exclamation mark) to indicate where it ends.
Consider these further examples:

1 Unless we receive payment within seven days, the service will be
discontinued.
2 Can England Avoid Defeat In Test Match?
3 Kindly refrain from smoking in the auditorium.
4 I Love New York!

Sentence 1 is a complex sentence which starts with a capital letter (<u>U</u>nless) and ends with a full stop (.).

Sentence 2 is a question which starts with a capital letter (<u>C</u>an) and ends with a question mark (?).

Sentence 3 gives an instruction which starts with a capital letter (<u>K</u>indly) and ends with a full stop.

Sentence 4 is an exclamation, which starts with a capital letter (<u>I</u>) and ends with an exclamation mark (!).

Activities 1 and 2

1 Read the following advertisement. Insert capital letters and full stops, question marks or exclamation marks where you think they are necessary.

Summertime and the living is easy. . .

even in Britain, summers can be very hot that's when ice-cream comes into its own we don't mean just any old ice-cream there are plenty of those around

so what ice-cream do we mean there's only one real ice-cream that will satisfy the ice-cream connoisseur

that's a SLIVER, the ice-cream bar of your fantasies it's coated with chocolate and filled with nuts the flavour is fabulous what other ice-cream can match it there's no other ice-cream within light years of SLIVER it's the ice-cream of the present and the future don't take our word for it after all, why should you we're trying to sell you something: the best ice-cream in the world

2 Read the following article. Full stops, capital letters, question marks and exclamation marks have been left out. Insert them where you think they are necessary.

Money

for many people, money is a real problem i don't mean not having enough of it, which clearly is a problem for lots of people, but money as an issue people get very confused and guilty about money why should this be so it has to be faced that money is a fact of life

many people say money is the root of all evil what a cop-out that is money is as good or as bad as the use you put it to why should money be seen as necessarily evil why should the pursuit of money be seen as necessarily bad yet often it is portrayed like that in books and films what hypocrisy that is

most people want to be wealthy at the very least, most people want to have more money than they have at present what is so wrong about that it's natural human instinct money can't buy happiness, but there are plenty of things it can buy believe me, I've been rich and I've been poor rich is better

WHERE ONE SENTENCE ENDS AND ANOTHER BEGINS

In your own writing, you have to know where one sentence ends and another begins.

Again, it is a matter of 'listening' to the sense of what you write. There is a flow of meaning that you must 'tune into'. This flow of meaning should tell you when one sentence ends and another begins. To illustrate this, read aloud the following passage, which is in the form of an office memorandum circulated to employees. The capital letters and full stops have been left out. As you read the words aloud, listen to the sense, the flow of meaning, and decide where one sentence naturally ends and another begins.

Availability of Tea and Coffee

Because of the difficulty of obtaining suitable part-time personnel and to cut down staffing costs, it has been decided to install a machine that dispenses hot drinks the machine, which will be situated on the second-floor landing, will offer tea, coffee, hot chocolate and soup the management has come to an agreement with the leasing firm that a certain amount of money will be earned by the machine every month this means we would like to encourage employees to use this facility after all, it is in your own best interests unfortunately, if a sufficient income is not earned through the sale of hot drinks, the agreement will have to be ended employees are also urged to keep the area clear of discarded plastic cups and other refuse any such occurrence will result in unnecessary costs for the company and make it more difficult for the arrangement to continue the co-operation of employees is earnestly requested

Having read it aloud, you will probably have identified natural 'resting places' in the flow of meaning (apart from those marked by commas, that is). Where a group of words make complete sense on their own (a statement is made, a question is asked or an expression of surprise, excitement, disgust, anger etc. is made), then you are reading a complete sentence. The natural sense of the above memorandum should have led you to this breakdown of 'separate' sentences:

1 Because of the difficulty . . . that dispenses hot drinks.
2 The machine . . . hot chocolate and soup.
3 The management . . . by the machine every month.
4 This means . . . this facility.
5 After all, it is . . . best interests.
6 Unfortunately . . . to be ended.
7 Employees are also urged . . . other refuse.
8 Any such occurrence . . . to continue.
9 The co-operation . . . requested.

It is important that you 'listen' to your own writing. If necessary, read what you have written aloud to yourself to 'hear' where one of your sentences naturally ends and another begins.

Ask yourself these questions about the sentences you write:

- Have I written a complete statement that makes sense on its own?
- Have I asked a direct question?
- Have I expressed an emotion of some kind that requires an exclamation mark?

✓ Checkpoint A

Read the following note. Listen to the 'voice' of the writer of the note and judge where one sentence should end and another begin. Rewrite the note appropriately.

I have been called away suddenly for an interview it's very exciting, isn't it I know you'll wish me luck it does mean I won't be back in time to go the theatre tonight the interview is in Nottingham and the earliest I'll be back in town is eight o'clock could I ask you to pick me up at the station that would be very nice of you, if you could we'd save on taxi fares as well why don't we eat together when I get back better still, we could get a take-away, our favourite Indian dishes, and that'll make up for not going to the theatre well, wish me luck I'll certainly need it I dont suppose I have any real chance of getting the job, but you never know one thing for sure, I'll be giving it my best shot see you this evening

Ian

3 Read the following letter aloud. Capital letters and full stops have been omitted. Judge by the sense where these should be inserted to indicate where sentences begin and end. Rewrite the letter appropriately.

Dear Sir

It has come to our attention that your current account was overdrawn last month by £25.40 as you know, facilities exist for current account holders to have arranged overdrafts our records show that you have not requested this facility

as is laid down in our conditions, a charge is levied on each transaction carried out during the period of an overdraft that has not been arranged we regret to inform you that a sum of £20 will be charged on November the 20th next to your current account to pay for the maintainance of the overdraft and for transactions since the overdraft occurred

if you wish to discuss this matter, please telephone the manager of the branch we would remind you, however, that it would be best to avoid this situation in the future by arranging prior overdraft facilities

Yours faithfully

G. Lament

4 Read the following monologue, aloud if possible. Describe where the speaker makes separate statements, asks questions or expresses emotion in an exclamation. Rewrite the monologue inserting the appropriate punctuation marks and capital letters.

You wouldn't believe how long I had to wait for a bus this afternoon there I was in the High Street in the pouring rain you know that shop that sells videos and things like that well, I was at the stop outside there it was pouring down and I didn't have an umbrella I couldn't shelter in the shop doorway because there was a big queue for the bus they're few and far between at the best of times and if you don't get on one, you have to wait ages, simply ages eventually the right bus comes along would you believe it two people got off and the conductor wouldn't allow anyone else on he said it was too crowded as it was I gave him a piece of my mind, I can tell you he wouldn't listen though he just drove off leaving this long queue standing in the rain do you know how long it took for the next bus to come along it was half-an-hour and then three came along at the same time it's always the way, isn't it you wait hours for a bus and then three come along at the same time it shouldn't be allowed

INCOMPLETE OR MINOR SENTENCES

So far we have been stressing the need to punctuate complete sentences correctly.

However, much of our spoken communication with one another is conducted in incomplete sentences. Using incomplete sentences can be appropriate when we are speaking, because it would be unnecessarily repetitive to use complete sentences all the time.

Consider this play extract:

INSPECTOR Where were you on the night of the 27th?
TED The 27th?
INSPECTOR Yes. Can't you remember? Strange.
TED Let me see. No. Nothing. Doesn't ring a bell.
INSPECTOR I suggest your memory takes a turn for the better.
TED Why?
INSPECTOR Because you're a suspect in this murder investigation.
TED Me?
INSPECTOR Yes, you, Mr Clark!
TED Ridiculous.
INSPECTOR Perhaps. The facts indicate otherwise.
TED The facts! What facts?
INSPECTOR Motive, Mr Clark. You had a motive.

Most of this conversation is conducted in incomplete sentences. These incomplete sentences are underlined.

These are sentence equivalents or **minor sentences**. They could have been expressed as complete sentences by the speakers (e.g. 'Where was I on the night of the 27th', 'Yes, that's what I mean' or 'Why do you say that?') but the context of the conversation allows for these incomplete sentences because it is clear what is meant.

Note, however, that these incomplete or minor sentences are punctuated in exactly the same way as complete sentences: they start with a capital letter and end with a full stop, question mark or exclamation mark.

In your own writing, you will normally use incomplete sentences only when you are putting down on the page the actual words people say (e.g. in story-telling).

However, there are some other occasions when incomplete sentences are appropriate, for example, if you are writing a short memo to someone. You want to keep it brief and concise so it might be appropriate to use incomplete sentences.

In a bit of rush. Have to go to meeting with suppliers. Back at 4. Would be nice if you could leave report of last meeting on my desk. Thanks for phoning those customers. Should get positive response. In all evening if I miss you this afternoon. Should be in at usual time tomorrow.

Jacqui

Note, too, that although this is an informal memo between people who obviously know each other well, the correct punctuation of the incomplete sentences aids clear communication.

Incomplete or minor sentences are appropriate in certain contexts. The important thing is for you to know when you are writing complete sentences and when you are deliberately choosing to write in incomplete sentences.

Activities 5,6 and 7

5 Read the following dialogue, which consists entirely of complete sentences. It is unnecessarily repetitive and could be improved by using incomplete sentences at times. Rewrite the passage using incomplete sentences where appropriate and provided that the meaning remains clear. Remember to punctuate these incomplete sentences correctly.

INTERVIEWER	But what is your attitude to this policy? Are you in agreement with it?
POLITICIAN	Of course, I am in agreement with the policy.
INTERVIEWER	Would you agree that some of your speeches seem to suggest that you have doubts?
POLITICIAN	I would not agree that some of my speeches seem to suggest that I have doubts. Are you suggesting otherwise?
INTERVIEWER	Yes, I am suggesting otherwise.
POLITICIAN	You are suggesting otherwise because it is your job to do so.
INTERVIEWER	Are you thinking of resigning from the government?
POLITICIAN	I am certainly not thinking of resigning from the government.
INTERVIEWER	Despite all the rumours, you are not thinking of resigning?
POLITICIAN	I am absolutely not thinking about resigning.

6 Read the following memo. It is written in incomplete sentences, but there is no punctuation. Rewrite the memo, inserting capital letters, full stops and question marks where appropriate.

have typed letters as requested have some queries have underlined relevant sections will be in office at 11 tomorrow loads of enquiries from advert seems to have paid off looking forward to dealing with all the letters I'll have to type hope your meeting went well.

7 Write brief notes or memos consisting of incomplete sentences appropriate for any of the following situations:
  a) You have decided to stay overnight at a friend's house. You leave a note for your parents explaining the situation.
  b) You have had some bad news about the serious illness of a relative. Your employer is out of the office and you decide to leave a note explaining why you have gone home and that you will probably be away from work for a few days.
  c) At work, you have taken several important phone calls for your boss while s/he has been out. You leave a memo with essential information about the calls.

COMMA-ITIS

One common mistake in punctuating sentences is to substitute commas for full stops.

This dependence on commas arises from a failure to recognise where one sentence ends and another begins. The writer realises that there is a pause in the flow of meaning but thinks a comma will cover it when in fact a full stop is required.

Read the following newspaper report. Frequently, commas have been used where full stops are required.

ENGLAND BATTLES FOR ASHES

England were facing heavy defeat in their struggle to regain the Ashes here in Melbourne, they were already two-nil down in the series. The third Test Match now seems to be drifting away from them, the most they can hope for is a draw. Despite a courageous innings by their captain, Spike Brotherton, England only managed a total of 366, this left them 153 runs behind Australia, there are two days left for play.

The writer of this report has suffered from 'comma-itis', which leads to over-dependence on commas at the cost of full stops. Reading the report aloud should tell you where the sense indicates that one sentence ends and another begins.

YES, I'M AFRAID THERE'S NO DOUBT ABOUT IT: YOU HAVE COMMA-ITIS.

England were facing heavy defeat in their struggle to regain the Ashes here in Melbourne. They were already two-nil down in the series. The third Test Match now seems to be drifting away from them. The most they can hope for is a draw. Despite a courageous innings by their captain, Spike Brotherton, England only managed a total of 366. This left them 153 runs behind Australia. There are two days left for play.

There are many times when commas should be used in punctuating a sentence. There will much more about commas in sentences in the next section of this book. However, you **never end a sentence with a comma** because that means you have failed to recognise where a sentence ends.

To illustrate how commas may be used correctly and incorrectly in sentences, read the following opening to a story:

The Creature
He wanted to create a creature, he wanted to be like a god and be a creator himself, he knew he had enough knowledge of biology and physics, because he had studied for many years at the feet of the greatest scientists in those fields, now he was ready to create a living being

Firstly, he had to have the raw materials that meant a human body, a corpse, in fact, there was no way round that, because he could not create human skin, a human brain and human organs, that was beyond even his powers, once he had those raw materials, he knew he could create a being, a creature who would be above all other beings.

The writer of this story has been struck with 'comma-itis'. Sometimes commas have been used correctly, but mostly they have been used as 'weak commas' that take the place of what should be full stops.

Before you read the corrected version below, re-read aloud the opening above and decide where these weak commas should be replaced by full stops.

He wanted to create a creature. He wanted to be like a god and be a creator himself. He knew he had enough knowledge of biology and physics, because he had studied for many years at the feet of the greatest scientists in those fields. Now he was ready to create a living being.

Firstly, he had to have the raw materials. That meant a human body, a corpse. In fact, there was no way round that, because he could not create human skin, a human brain and human organs. That was beyond even his powers. Once he had those raw materials, he knew he could create a being, a creature who would be above all other beings.

Now the story is correctly punctuated. 'Comma-itis' has been banished and strong full stops to mark a definite stop in the flow of meaning have replaced the weak commas. Some commas remain, however, correctly placed in the story, because they mark only a slight pause in the flow of meaning.

'Comma-itis' is a very common fault, so be aware of this when you are writing. Check your sentences and decide when one ends and another begins by either reading them aloud 'in your head' or by actually reading them aloud.

✓ *Checkpoint B*

Read the following letter written by a young person seeking employment. Once again the writer has been afflicted with 'comma-itis'. Decide which commas have incorrectly taken the place of full stops or question marks.

Dear Sir/Madam

I am writing to enquire whether you have any vacancies at present in your firm, I am sixteen years of age and have just left school.

I have several passes at GCSE level including a 'B' grade in English and Maths, my final school report is also excellent, I can also supply references from my former headmistress and past employers.

Is there any chance of my being able to make an appointment to come and see you to discuss employment prospects, I live very close to your firm so travelling to and from work would not be a problem, my family have had a past connection with your firm, I would very much like to work for Druid Engineering, I hope that this enquiry is of some interest to you, I look forward to hearing from you,

Yours faithfully

Lucy Cooper

Activity 3

Continue the story 'The Creature' in your own way, making sure that you punctuate the sentences you write correctly and avoiding any sign of 'comma-itis'.

SKILLCHECK Check these statements to assess what you have learnt from this section. If you cannot honestly tick all of these statements, then go back over the relevant section.

❑ I can differentiate between a complete sentence and an incomplete sentence.

❑ I know that sentences need a capital letter at the start and a full stop, question or exclamation mark at the end.

❑ I understand when it is appropriate to use incomplete sentences.

❑ I am aware of the danger of 'comma-itis'.

2
COMMAS

WHEN TO USE COMMAS

In the final part of the previous section, it was stressed that a comma should never take the place of, or try to do the work of, a full stop.

Anyone who has ever marked examination papers will tell you that one of the commonest errors candidates make is inserting too many commas instead of full stops.

This is such a major error that it is worth starting this section of the book with another reminder about this 'comma-itis'.

When you are writing, try to 'hear' the sentences. Say them in your head and decide where the sense dictates that one sentence ends and another begins. Those are the places where you need full stops, **not** commas.

YOUR TROUBLE IS YOU THINK YOU'RE A FULL STOP WHEN YOU'RE ONLY A COMMA!

Read aloud the following piece of writing about someone's summer holiday. There are some commas that have been used correctly and some that have been used incorrectly. The 'incorrect' commas are trying to do the work of full stops.

The weather was absolutely delightful, despite my fears about it being too hot, I don't much like beach holidays, but I have to say that this summer holiday was really special, there was so much else to do anyway apart from lying on the beach, for example, there were ancient ruins to visit, great art galleries, some theme parks and, of course, wonderful discos, which went on till the early hours of the morning, I met some interesting people of my own age from other countries, the language barrier was a problem at first, but it was fun trying out the few words of French and German I knew already, a lot of them spoke English, which helped.

This is the correct version divided up into numbered sentences:

1 The weather was absolutely delightful, despite my fears about it being too hot.
2 I don't much like beach holidays, but I have to say that this summer holiday was really special.
3 There was so much else to do anyway apart from lying on the beach.
4 For example, there were ancient ruins to visit, great art galleries, some theme parks and, of course, wonderful discos, which went on till the early hours of the morning.
5 I met some interesting people of my own age from other countries.
6 The language barrier was a problem at first, but it was fun trying out the few words of French and German I knew already.
7 A lot of them spoke English, which helped.

The flow of meaning should have told you when one complete statement had been made and, therefore, a full stop was required.

Note, however, how some commas have been retained in the corrected sentences. Only the commas that were wrongly 'standing in' for full stops have been removed.

In sentence 1, the comma after *delightful* indicates a pause between the description of the weather and the rest of the sentence. The comma marks this pause.

Sentence 2 has two main parts or clauses joined by the 'joining word' *but*. It is usual to put a comma after the first main clause in a compound sentence like this when *but* is the joining word.

Sentence 3 has no need of a comma.

Sentence 4 has a comma after *For example* because there is a definite pause which needs to be marked between that phrase and the rest of the sentence. Then commas separate the list of interesting things to do and they 'surround' the phrase *of course*. A comma is placed before the second clause starting with *which*.

Sentence 5 has no need of a comma.

Sentence 6 is a similar sentence to sentence 2.

Sentence 7 has a comma before the second clause.

These sentences illustrate some of the uses of commas that we will be exploring in the rest of the section.

The important thing to remember is that sentences do sometimes need commas, but never at the end. The secret of how to avoid using commas instead of full stops is to know when a sentence has been completed.

✓ *Checkpoint A*

Read the following piece of writing about someone's favourite television series. There are no full stops because the writer has allowed one sentence to flow into another with only commas to separate them. Read the passage aloud and decide where the sentences end and where full stops are required. Some commas have been used correctly.

'Star Trek', both the old series and the 'new generation' adventures, is my favourite television series, I love the characters, the plots, the sets and everything about the series, Captain Kirk, Mr Spock, Scottie and a host of other characters have become like real people to me, despite the fact that I know they are only imaginary and have never lived, of course, I am not alone in enjoying this fantasy, because there are 'Trekkies' all over the world

    Indeed, the fans of the series are avid collectors of everything to do with the programme, serious collectors will buy anything to do with the series: annuals, autographs of the stars, props, publicity material, 'Star Trek' represents for me, and for many other people, I guess, an alternative reality, a way of escaping into the unknown, which is harmless and enjoyable, the episodes often have a serious point, however, they are not very violent and usually have some kind of moral message to them, mostly I watch them for the weird effects and the unlikely adventures in space, the aliens they encounter, as they boldly go where no man has gone before, are also always fascinating, it is a great show.

THE NEED FOR COMMAS

Look at these three notes:

1 Ben my uncle has died. Have had to go to funeral.
2 Ben, my uncle has died. Have had to go to funeral.
3 Ben, my uncle, has died. Have had to go to funeral.

To someone who did not know anything about the context, note 1 would be confusing. Is the note addressing Ben and informing the recipient that an uncle has died or does the note say that the writer's uncle called Ben has died? It is not clear.

    However, notes 2 and 3 communicate clearly because of the addition of commas.

    In note 2, the comma after *Ben* indicates that the note is addressed to Ben and the information is that the writer's uncle has died.

    In note 3, the commas after *Ben* and after *uncle* indicate that Ben and the uncle are one and the same person. The phrase *my uncle* is **in parenthesis** to Ben. In other words, the phrase explains who Ben is.

Here is another example:

As soon as the red light flashes drive.

It is not absolutely clear what this notice means. However, the addition of a comma makes all clear:

As soon as the red light flashes, drive.

Here is another confusing notice:

Immediately you hear the bell ring.

The addition of a comma clears up any doubt about the meaning:

Immediately you hear the bell, ring.

A comma marks a short pause in the flow of meaning, but the omission of a comma can cause confusion and poor communication.

Activity 1

Read the following note. The writer has left out essential commas that would make the meaning much clearer. Rewrite the note twice with different use of commas that will result in different meanings.

Sherry my cat has just had kittens. Would you like one of them? Janet my mate at the office has said she'll have one, but if you hurry, you can still have the pick of the litter. Immediately you see her choose. They'll go fast. Sherry my favourite animal must be rewarded for her efforts! It's only the best for her from now on.

SUBORDINATE CLAUSES

1 Keep off the grass.
2 Write the reference number of your account here and sign below.
3 When the red light flashes, apply the hand-brake.

All the above signs are sentences that give instructions.

Sentence 1 is a simple sentence. It consists of one main or independent clause and makes sense on its own. It has no need for commas.

Sentence 2 is a compound or double sentence: it consists of two main or independent clauses that could be written as separate sentences, but in this compound sentence they are joined together by *and*. In this type of compound sentence, no comma is required between the two parts of the sentence.

Sentence 3 is a complex sentence: it consists of a main or independent clause, plus another clause. The main clause is *apply the hand-brake.* Those words could stand on their own and make sense. The rest of the sentence *When the red light flashes* does not make sense on its own. It is subordinate to (i.e. it depends on) the main clause. It is usual to place a comma between the subordinate clause and the main clause.

Here are other examples of complex sentences where a comma is usually required between the main clause and subordinate clauses.

The management cannot be held responsible for customers' belongings, although every effort will be made to look after them.

Supporters are asked to refrain from obscenities, because such behaviour easily causes offence.

In each of these examples, a comma separates the two parts of the sentence. If you read them aloud, you will notice a natural pause between these two parts: that is where the comma should be placed.

In compound or double sentences, if the conjunction or joining word is **but,** it is usual to separate the two main clauses with a comma, as in these newspaper headlines:

GOVERNMENT HOLDS SEAT, BUT IT'S CLOSE

SCOTLAND WIN, BUT IT'S DULL!

MARRIAGE IS ROCKY, BUT THERE'S HOPE

Activity 2

Read the following newspaper report. Insert commas where you think they are necessary to clarify meaning.

EAGLES WIN BUT IT'S HARD WORK!

The Springfield Eagles struggled to record a 1-0 victory over a weak home team today although they dominated for much of the game. The 12,000 crowd were treated to a determined effort from both teams but there was little to lighten the wintry gloom. When the Eagles went into the lead after twelve minutes home supporters probably expected an avalanche of goals as the Beavers have one of the worst defensive records in the league. However, it was not to be and the Eagles had to be content with the narrowest of victories.

The approach play of the home team was a delight to watch but the killer instinct was sadly lacking in the end. Although the manager made two late substitutions it made no difference to the striking power and two late chances for the Beavers even put the result in doubt. The victory is very welcome as the Eagles keep up their late challenge to head the league.

DEFINING AND NON-DEFINING CLAUSES

Compare these two very similar sentences:

The survivors who were hurt and suffering from exposure were brought on board.
The survivors, who were hurt and suffering from exposure, were brought on board.

Here the insertion of commas or the absence of commas makes a difference to the meaning.

In the first sentence, the absence of commas implies that **only** the survivors who were hurt and suffering from exposure were brought on board.

In the second sentence, the commas that separate the clause *who were hurt and suffering from exposure* from the main clause tell us that this is additional information about the survivors, but it does not **define** which survivors they were. It gives extra information about (all) the survivors.

Here are other examples:

The spectators, who had paid a lot for their tickets, were given top priority.
The spectators who had paid a lot for their tickets were given top priority.

In the first sentence the clause *who had paid a lot for their tickets* gives additional information about the spectators, but it does not define a particular group from among them. This is made clear by the commas round the clause.

In the second sentence the same clause defines which group of spectators are meant: only those who had paid a lot for their tickets, not any other spectators. Therefore, no commas are used.

These examples illustrate how the use or absence of commas affects meaning. Be clear in your mind about whether or not you are defining a particular group when you write sentences like these. If you are, then commas should not be used.

✓ *Checkpoint B*

Some of these sentences have clauses which define a particular group. Others have clauses which do not define a group, but which give additional information about all involved. Decide which clauses are defining and which are non-defining.

1 The travellers who had been delayed were dealt with first.

2 The gamblers, who were excited and noisy, expected to win heavily.

3 Although the dogs that had been in quarantine looked despondent, the cats seemed healthy and fit.

4 Mothers who accompanied their children were allowed in free of charge.

5 Mothers, who accompanied their children, were allowed in free of charge.

6 Even those critics who hated the film praised its technical virtuosity.

PHRASES WITH PARTICIPLES

Consider the following examples:

Whistling cheerfully, he left the house.
Before boarding the train, passengers must purchase a ticket.
Having refused to lower taxes, the government is now highly unpopular.
The prisoners, **having failed to escape**, surrendered.
Before lifting the receiver, insert the required money in the box.

In each case, the part of the sentence printed in bold type is separated from the rest of the sentence by a comma or a pair of commas. Phrases such as *having failed to escape, before boarding the train* and *whistling cheerfully* all contain a **participle** – the part of the verb ending in -ing. When phrases such as these appear at the beginning or in the middle of a sentence, a comma or a pair of commas separates the participial phrase from the main clause of the sentence.

The rule, as before, is that commas are used to mark a pause in the flow of meaning and to divide one unit of sense from another unit.

Activity 3

Read the following report. Commas that are necessary have been omitted.
Rewrite the passage inserting commas appropriately.

Annual College Report

Student numbers having reached a peak during last year substantially decreased this year. Whilst anticipating a small decrease in student enrolment the college administration are disappointed with the size of the decrease.

Having decided to offer even more vocational courses this year the director of education expected these to attract substantial numbers. Making the judgement that vocational courses were what students wanted he authorised expenditure on several new subject areas.

Having failed to meet the targets for student numbers this year staff have been asked to redouble their efforts in the next few months. Considering the economic situation of the college it is more important than ever for administration staff to cooperate with teachers to produce more students for courses next year.

COMMAS AND LISTS

Elizabeth Taylor
Meryl Streep
Kathleen Turner
Susan Sarandon
Michelle Pfeiffer

COFFEE
TEA
FISH FINGERS
BREAD
REFUSE BAGS

Cats
Sunset Boulevard
Crazy For You
Les Misérables

Above are three lists of various things. If a list is employed in a sentence, commas have to be used to separate the various items. If you do not use commas, the reader has more difficulty in making sense of it. One other point about lists: the last two items in the list are joined by and, so no comma is required:

Among the actresses being considered for the part are Elizabeth Taylor, Meryl Streep, Kathleen Turner, Susan Sarandon and Michelle Pfeiffer.

Note how the last two names in the list are joined by *and* and how commas separate the other names in the list.

Without commas the second list would look like this:

Please buy coffee tea refuse bags fish fingers and bread.

I'D LIKE TWO EGGS, BACON, SAUSAGES, FRIED TOMATOES, FRIED BREAD, HASH BROWNS, BLACK PUDDING AND CHIPS!

The reader would have difficulty in making sense of this: does *fingers* belong with *fish* or is it a separate item, for example? Commas and the final joining *and*, however, clear up any doubts:

Please buy coffee, tea, refuse bags, fish fingers and bread.

The third list would look like this in a sentence:

Tonight we have tickets available for 'Cats', 'Sunset Boulevard', 'Crazy For You' and 'Les Misérables'.

Activity 4

Read the following article. It uses several lists, but the commas have been missed out. Rewrite the article inserting commas where you think they are appropriate.

Nursery nurses require patience understanding stamina skills and an innate love of children. Trainees will be assessed on their practical skills knowledge of child psychology ability to work with other people and their commitment to the job. Qualifications in English social studies psychology and nursing are required. Successful trainees can look forward to a career that offers job satisfaction secure employment prospects opportunities for promotion and a good salary.

COMMAS AND ADJECTIVES, ADVERBS AND VERBS

In the examples given above, all the lists consist of nouns. Adjectives, adverbs and verbs can come in the form of lists as well.

A sure-fire, crackling, stupendous hit!

Magical, Tantalising and Mysterious!

These newspaper quotes about shows use three adjectives one after the other. In the first, a comma separates the first from the second adjective, and another comma separates the second from the third. In the second headline, a comma separates the first two adjectives, but the second and third adjectives are joined by *and* so no comma is required.

However, sometimes two adjectives naturally belong together and do not need to be separated by a comma:

Darling, I thought I'd wear my <u>bright pink</u> trouser suit tonight.
The Prime Minister wore a <u>charcoal grey</u> suit with a <u>light blue</u> shirt.

Adverbs can also be used in strings:

Giggs plays football joyously, inventively and gracefully, as it should be played.
Steffi Graf won the final emphatically, skilfully and graciously.

Note the commas that separate the first two adverbs and the final *and*.
Verbs, too, can be used in a list of actions:

At Wembley Arena last night, the NosePickers were cheered, adored, enthroned and raised to the status of idols.
In this role, Dame Juliet Tench rages, cries, erupts and finally convinces us that she is a great actress.

Commas separate the individual verbs until the final pair when *and* is used.

Activity 5

Read the following newspaper account of a rock concert. Insert commas only when you think they are appropriate.

OLD ROCKERS NEVER DIE

Purple Flood, the oldest rockers in the business, wowed mesmerised excited and startled their loyal audience at Ibrox last night. The Flood were greeted rapturously deliriously and, I have to say, hysterically by thousands of Glaswegians in the huge awe-inspiring modern stadium.

The fans cheered stamped their feet yelled their heads off swayed in unison and generally did a fair imitation of your average rock concert audience. The ancient Flood, now all in their sixties, were distant cool regal and unaffected, as befits rock stars of their stature. Methodically painstakingly and seemingly endlessly, the group played their way through their list of greatest hits such as 'One More Million in the Bank' 'The Garden Wall' 'Leave the Drugs Alone' and 'Geriatric Rock'. Roger Dodger, the sixty-five-year-old lead singer, wore a bright cerise leather outfit, which most fans pronounced glamorous sexy and unique.

COMMAS AND INTERJECTIONS/ASIDES

An interjection or an aside is a word or phrase that expresses a feeling of surprise, anger, joy and other emotions, doubt or emphasis.

If an interjection/aside comes at the beginning of a sentence or phrase, then it should be followed by a comma, as in these examples:

Oh, I didn't really expect this to happen.
Well, that takes the biscuit!
Of course, her success came as no surprise to me.

If the interjection comes in the middle of a sentence, then it should be 'surrounded' by commas:

The government will, naturally, pay the bill.
The book will, of course, sell in millions.
The jury intend, without doubt, to find him innocent.

A comma is also required when 'yes' or 'no' is used at the beginning of sentences as a part of an answer:

Yes, we have no bananas!
No, we have no bananas!

Activity 6

Read the following dialogue from a play. Decide where commas have been omitted incorrectly and rewrite the dialogue inserting them where it is appropriate.

JIM **Hey give me a break!**

JOAN **No why should I?**

JIM **Indeed why should you? We're only old friends that's all.**

JOAN **Really you could have fooled me.**

JIM **Of course you won't tell me what I'm supposed to have done.**

JOAN **No naturally I won't.**

JIM **Great thanks very much.**

JOAN **Oh don't be so sarcastic.**

JIM **Well what do you expect? Understanding?**

JOAN **As a matter of fact yes I do.**

COMMAS IN LETTER-WRITING

In the layout of the details at the top of a letter, it is possible not to use any commas. This is particularly true of more formal letters that use a block format as in the following example:

Midas Bank
65 Threadbare Street
London EC1 2YD

29 July 1998

Cynthia Butcher
25 Rainforest Road
Broughton
BR1 6NL

Dear Ms Butcher

You may remember that you wrote to us. . .

The letter then follows a block paragraphing format with no indentation from the margin for new paragraphs. The closing would be as follows:

Yours sincerely

Louise B. Hartley

L. B. Hartley
Finance Manager

However, for less formal letters and especially letters that are handwritten, another format is normally used where commas are definitely required. Each use of a comma in the layout of this letter is underlined:

```
                                          14, Belsize Avenue,
                                           Templeton, TN3 8RT
                                           29 November 1998


Dear Sammy,
   I was very pleased to receive your recent letter and I. . .
```

A letter using this kind of format would indent from the margin for each new paragraph and punctuate the closing:

```
                    With best wishes,



                    John Ray
```

Note where commas have been underlined in the layout of this letter:
- The sender's address: at the end of the line giving the number of house and road name; after the name of the town.
- Date (below the sender's address): after the month.
- The greeting or mode of address: after the person's name.
- Closing or signing off: after the signing off (in this example *With best wishes* because the person is addressed by name in the greeting).

Of course, there will be other places in the course of a letter where commas must be used, as in other contexts, but here we are emphasising the need to use commas in setting out letters (except when you use block paragraphing format).

Activity 7

Read the following personal letter. Commas have been omitted in the layout of the letter. Rewrite the letter inserting the missing commas where necessary in the layout and also in other places where you think they have been omitted.

> 65 Charnel Lane
> Middletown MT1 2RF
>
> Dear Dorothy
>
> I thought I had to write to you to tell you of my surprise joy and excitement about the GCSE exams. Yes I mean how many good grades I managed.
>
> Maths biology French English history science and social studies were my successes and only in geography German and drama was I really disappointed. Well I was really excited when I received those results I can tell you.
>
> Naturally I'm very interested to hear how you got on. Please write to me as soon as possible with your news. I hope of course that you've done as well as I have.
>
> Love
>
> Karen

SKILLCHECK   Check these statements to assess what you have learnt from this section. If you cannot honestly tick all of these statements, then go back over the relevant section.

❏ I can use commas to mark a slight pause in the flow of meaning and help to separate one unit of sense from another.

❏ I am aware of the dangers of 'comma-itis', particularly the use of commas instead of full stops to separate sentences.

❏ I realise that by missing out necessary commas I could be making it difficult for my readers to understand clearly what I have written.

❏ I know how to use commas to separate subordinate clauses from main clauses.

❏ I understand how commas should be used in laying out a letter.

3
PUNCTUATING SPEECH

DIRECT AND INDIRECT SPEECH

Read the following newspaper headlines:

'I Was Duped!' Claims Duchess

'WE WERE ROBBED!' SAYS ENGLAND MANAGER

'The Worst Case I Have Ever Tried!' Says Judge

Prime Minister Claims 'Government Is On Steady Course'

All these headlines **quote** the actual words someone has said. What has been recorded are the words the people spoke.

Notice how those words or **direct speech** are surrounded by **speech marks** (also known as **inverted commas**).

Be clear in your own mind about the difference between direct speech and **indirect speech**, sometimes referred to as **reported speech**. Indirect speech or reported speech reports what someone has said, but may not write down the actual words he or she has used. For example, if the above headlines had been expressed in indirect or reported speech, they would look like this:

Duchess Claims She Was Duped!

ENGLAND MANAGER SAYS THEY WERE ROBBED

Judge Says Worst Case He Has Ever Tried!

Prime Minister Claims Government Is On Steady Course

Reported or indirect speech does not require inverted commas or speech marks.

✓ Checkpoint A

Which of the following use direct speech and which use reported or indirect speech?

1 Minister Says He Will Sue Newspaper
2 The teacher said that the essays has to be in by Tuesday.
3 Coroner Finds 'Much To Be Concerned About'
4 'There is no truth in these rumours. We are just good friends.'
5 She said that she would be in touch in the new year.
6 'I've grown accustomed to her face,' he said.

SINGLE OR DOUBLE INVERTED COMMAS?

You have a choice of using single inverted commas ('. . .') or double inverted commas (". . ."). Both are acceptable, although it is important not to mix them up within one piece of writing. If you start using single inverted commas in a piece of writing, continue to use single throughout. Similarly, if you start using double inverted commas, continue with these throughout.

When you are quoting from a book or some other source, or mention the title of a film, programme or book etc., it is usual to use single inverted commas:

> 'Gone With The Wind' is the most successful film in film history.
> 'Coronation Street' is the world's longest-running soap opera.

The only time you use single and double in one piece of writing is when you quote the title of something, or quote something someone has said, within direct speech itself. That is where the alternative use of single or double inverted commas comes in useful. If you are using single inverted commas round the direct speech, then the quotation can be indicated within double inverted commas:

> 'I love the Belchers record "No One Likes Us, We Don't Care". It's great,' she said.

In the above example of direct speech which has employed single inverted commas, the title of a record is mentioned within the direct speech and this is indicated by the double inverted commas round the title.

> "Shakespeare wrote this line: 'Shall I compare thee to a summer's day?' Isn't that lovely?"

In this example, the direct speech is enclosed within double inverted commas and the quotation is, therefore, indicated by single inverted commas.

When you use direct speech in a piece of your writing, make up your mind whether you are going to use single or double inverted commas. If you quote someone's words, or refer to the title of something within the direct speech, then use single commas if you have started with double, and vice versa.

Activity 1

Below are several examples of direct speech. Make up your mind whether to use single or double inverted commas round the direct speech. Rewrite the passages using inverted commas, remembering to use single or double inverted commas as appropriate when a quotation is made within the direct speech or when the title of something is referred to.

a Was it John Donne who wrote, No man is an island? she asked.

b I can't remember the name of the movie. Maybe it was Plan Nine From Outer Space or Brain From Mars. Anyway, it was decidedly the worst movie I've ever seen. And that includes The Sound of Music, he added.

c On the syllabus this term are Of Mice and Men, Sons and Lovers, Great Expectations and On the Black Hill, said the teacher.

d Can I quote you what the Prime Minister actually said? She said, Where there was war, let there be peace. That's what she said.

e Let's go and see that movie, what's it called? Exterminator 27. Let me quote you what the newspaper critic said. A must for all action fans, a mind-blowing cinematic experience. There you are. Let's go.

THE PUNCTUATION OF DIRECT SPEECH

Read this opening to a science fiction story. Important points to do with the punctuation of direct speech are numbered (1)–(16).

Duke Stargoer gazed across the vast, empty plains of the iceberg plant.
(1) 'This is not a warm place, Louie,' (2) he said.
Louie, a fine example of the Dookie species, grunted.
(3) 'You don't say, Louie. You too, eh?' (4) said Stargoer in reply.
(5) 'Erhhhhhh! Frrrrrr!' (6) uttered Louie.
(7) 'I couldn't agree more,' (8) replied Duke. (9) 'The Consortium want us here so here we'll stay for a while. Until we've found the evil Grunga, at least.' (10)
(11) 'Grrrrrrrr!' (12) growled Louie.
(13) 'Don't whine, Louie. You Dookies are a fine species, but you do whine a lot,' (14) said Duke.
Louie looked at him and kept his thoughts to himself.
(15) 'I can see that remark made me unpopular.' (16)

The first example of direct speech is (1) and (2):

'This is not a warm place, Louie,' he said.

(1) This sentence uses single inverted commas and starts with a capital letter at the first word (*This*). The first word within speech marks always starts with a capital letter **except** when the speech is interrupted by a 'he said' or something similar and the speech continues within the same sentence.
(2) When a stretch of spoken words comes to an end, there must be a punctuation mark before the closing inverted commas. In . . . *Louie,' he said*, notice that the comma is placed inside the inverted comma, not outside it.

The second example of direct speech is (3) and (4):

'You don't say, Louie. You too, eh?' said Stargoer in reply.

(3) Again, a single inverted comma indicates the start of direct speech. The first word has a capital letter.
(4) When this stretch of speech comes to an end, the punctuation mark is a question mark because a question has been asked. Note again that this is placed inside the closing inverted comma.

The third example of direct speech is (5) and (6):

'Erhhhhhh! Frrrrrr!' uttered Louie.

(5) Open inverted commas, capital letter for first word.
(6) Exclamation mark this time before closing inverted comma.

The fourth example is a more extended piece of direct speech (7), (8), (9) and (10):

'I couldn't agree more,' replied Duke. 'The consortium want us here so here we stay for a while. Until we've found the evil Grunga, at least.'

(7) Open inverted commas, capital letter.
(8) Comma before closing inverted comma.
(9) Open inverted commas, capital letter.
(10) Full stop before closing inverted comma.

The fifth example of direct speech is (11) and (12).
(11) Open inverted commas, capital letter.
(12) Exclamation mark before the closing inverted comma.

The sixth example is (13) and (14).
(13) Open inverted commas, capital letter.
(14) Comma before closing inverted comma.

The last example, (15) and (16) is different in that the sentence finishes with the end of the direct speech. In this situation, the punctuation mark that comes before the closing inverted comma is a full stop.

Activity 2

Read the continuation of the above story. Punctuation of direct speech has been omitted, as well as some capital letters. Rewrite the passage, punctuating the direct speech correctly.

Duke donned his special telescopic glasses.

There's something moving out there, he said. I can't quite make it out yet. It must be about two thousand miles away.

Louie made a restless sound.

Patience, Louie, Duke said, you'll get your chance for action.

Droonggg? howled Louie.

How do I know? Duke retorted. You daft Dookie! not psychic.

calling Duke Stargoer! calling Duke Stargoer! Someone was calling him on his interplanetary mobile.

yeh? This is Stargoer. Who's calling? Over.

Who do you think's calling, you chump? This is Fran Solitaire.

Solitaire! Have they got you back in harness? replied Duke.

For a price, said Solitaire, only for a high price.

Same old Fran, replied Duke. You never do anything for nothing.

INTERRUPTED DIRECT SPEECH

Sometimes, as we have seen above, the actual words spoken by someone, and written down on the page, are in the form of a sentence, which is **interrupted** by the words that indicate the speaker, e.g. she said, he retorted, they demanded.

When this is the case, and you are sure that the sentence has been interrupted, you have to be careful about the punctuation:

(1)' (2) We are hoping for a cessation of violence, (3)' (4) said the UN spokesperson, (5)' (6) (7) but we cannot promise it. (8)' (9)

This piece of direct speech is punctuated like this:

(1) opening inverted comma
(2) capital letter

(3) comma before the closing inverted comma
(4) closing inverted comma
(5) a comma after the interruption
(6) open inverted commas again to indicate direct speech
(7) small, lower case letter and **not** a capital letter because it is still the same sentence
(8) full stop at the end of the direct speech because nothing else follows it
(9) close inverted commas

If you are uncertain whether the direct speech quoted does consist of one sentence, then read it aloud without the interruption and judge whether it makes sense on its own:

'I am hoping for the best,' she said, 'but who knows what will happen?'

If you ignore the *she said*, the direct speech makes sense on its own as a complete sentence: *I am hoping for the best, but who knows what will happen?* Note the punctuation, especially the comma after the interruption and the small letter after the inverted commas have been opened again.

Very often, however, the interruption comes between separate, complete sentences, which demands this kind of punctuation pattern:

'The train standing at platform seven is the 5.30 to Brighton,' said the station announcer. 'We apologise for the late departure of this train.'

Here the two parts of the direct speech, separated by *said the station announcer*, are clearly separate sentences. Therefore, the second sentence must be treated exactly like the first part with a capital letter after the opening inverted comma.

Sometimes the interruption comes at the start of the direct speech:

He asked, 'What do you mean by that?'
She said sadly, 'I don't understand it at all.'
They demanded angrily, 'Give us back our money.'

With this pattern of direct speech, note the comma after the interruption and the capital letter at the first word of the direct speech.

✓ *Checkpoint B*

Read the following aloud and decide whether they are examples of interrupted complete sentences or not.

1 The flight has been cancelled said the tour guide the fog is too dense.

2 I will never forgive you for this she said because I feel I have been betrayed.

3 Of course, the company will pay all expenses he added as you will have to be away from home.

4 Never cross the road against the lights the instructor said it is highly dangerous.

Activity 3

Read the following opening to a story. The direct speech has been left unpunctuated. Rewrite the passage inserting the appropriate punctuation.

Take a seat Farlowe said I didn't catch the name.

I didn't throw it the woman said you may call me Mrs Amstrad.

May I indeed? said Farlowe in his most biting tone that's just grand.

Am I speaking to Mr Dick Farlowe, private detective the woman asked.

If you're not, you've come to the wrong office Farlowe replied and I don't know who I am.

Does anyone of us know who we are replied the visitor.

Ah, a philosopher said Farlowe I've always wanted to meet one.

Well, now you have said the woman I have a job for you, Mr Farlowe.

Times are bad said Farlowe and I could use the business.

Never advertise yourself as unsuccessful, Mr Farlowe Mrs Amstrad said it's not good for your business which isn't good in the first place no one wants to employ a failure.

I can see you're not only a philosopher but a psychologist as well Farlowe said coolly have you any other talents

None that would interest you she replied

Try me said Farlowe you might surprise yourself and me

PARAGRAPHING IN DIRECT SPEECH

The rule about paragraphs and direct speech is that you need to start a new paragraph each time the speaker changes. Consider this example:

'How are you today, Edna?' said Rena brightly.

'Not so bad,' Edna replied. 'Aches and pains, you know the sort of thing. Comes with middle-age.'

'Doesn't it just? You never think you're going to get old when you're young, do you? You think it will go on forever. That your health will hold out and you'll be different.'

'Right.'

'Yes, you don't know anything when you're young,' said Rena.

Notice how in this passage of direct speech a new paragraph is begun each time the conversation changes hands. You start a new paragraph by **indenting** from the margin. If you do not do this with direct speech, then it becomes much more difficult for your reader to make sense of what you have written.

Even when a speaker says something very brief, even one word, and then someone else takes over, you should indicate this change by starting a new paragraph. Read this continuation of the conversation above; this time there is no paragraphing.

'No.' 'Well, you live and. . .' 'Learn. That's right.' 'Yes, that's right,' said Rena. 'You can't put an old head on young shoulders.' 'No, you can't.' 'You can tell them, but they don't listen,' said Rena. 'No, they don't listen.' 'No, they don't listen.'

Now it is not at all clear who is saying what when. This lack of clarity is cleared up, however, if a new paragraph is started each time this conversation changes hands:

'No.'
'Well, you live and. . .'
'Learn. That's right.'
'Yes, that's right,' said Rena. 'You can't put an old head on young shoulders.'
'No, you can't.'
'You can tell them, but they don't listen,' said Rena.
'No, they don't listen.'
'No, they don't listen.'

The Jane Austen School of Creative Writing

Student authors are reminded they must start a new paragraph each time a conversation changes hands in their stories. Failure to comply with this rule will lead to an immediate fine of having to read the complete collected works of an extremely boring author.

This rule about paragraphing is the same when there are more than two speakers in the conversation:

'I want to recall the witness Field,' said the defending counsel.
'I object,' interrupted the prosecutor.
'Why exactly do you object, Mr Mason?' asked the judge wearily.
'Because he likes objecting,' said Adams, the defending counsel.
'The defence lawyer had his chance to cross-examine this witness yesterday,' the prosecutor said. 'Why should he recall the witness?'
'Why should he not, Mr Mason? Objection overruled,' said the judge.
'Thank you, my lord.'

Notice, too, how frequently the speaker is identified in the 'interruption'. This, together with the paragraphing, helps the reader make sense of the direct speech.

4 Read the following opening to a story. The conversation is between two people, but there is no paragraphing to help the reader. Rewrite the passage inserting the appropriate punctuation and paragraphing.

So when did you stumble across the body asked Leila Brogan. Who wants to know replied the old man. Oh, sorry, my name is Leila Brogan. I'm a detective. You're a what asked the old man incredulously. A detective said Leila. Of the private kind. Like in them books? Yes, like in them books replied Leila. Now at what time did you discover the dead body. I can't remember. Anyway, I've told all this to the police who came. Well, tell me again. Why should I said the old man. You're not the police. No, I'm not replied Leila patiently but I've been asked by the family to look into this murder. Murder! Who said it was murder the old man erupted. All right, then, a death in mysterious circumstances. Now what time did you come across this body that died in these mysterious circumstances? I don't need to talk to you said the old man. You can't force me to. That's true sighed Leila but I just thought you might want to help and to clear yourself of any suspicion. What do you mean by that exploded the old man.

5 The following opening to a story has direct speech involving four different speakers. Once again, there is no paragraphing to help the reader. Rewrite the passage starting new paragraphs where you think they are appropriate and inserting any missing punctuation marks.

Tell me, Mr Vincent said Lady Hawke haughtily where do your family come from? Shropshire said Vincent. Indeed said Lady Hawke I don't recall any Vincents from Shropshire. Really, Mummy, don't be such a snob interjected Emily. I'm sure there's nothing wrong with his family. One must be so careful these days, said Lady Hawke. I say, steady on, old gal intervened Lord Hawke twentieth-century and all that, you know. I simply want to marry your daughter said Vincent. Simply exclaimed Lady Hawke Simply he says. And I want to marry him said Emily. We'll see about that shouted Lady Hawke. Yes, we shall said Emily. Let's not have a row said Lord Hawke. Why not said Emily it's about time we had a jolly good row in this family. I don't want to cause any dissension said Vincent. Well, it seems you have, doesn't it said Lady Hawke. I love your daughter, Lady Hawke, that's the end of the story. Oh, no, it isn't, not by a long chalk exploded Lady Hawke. I'll have your family investigated. Really, Mummy, this is just too much said Emily. Yes, my dear, steady on said his lordship. There is a limit, you know. Not for me said Lady Hawke. I will go right over the top.

USING INDIRECT SPEECH

In any narrative you write (e.g. when you are writing fiction in the form of short stories, or when you are writing an autobiographical piece based on your own experience), you may well want to use direct speech.

In more formal writing, however, direct speech is generally inappropriate, but you may want to **report** what someone has said in a piece of writing. Reported or indirect speech, as has already been pointed out, does not require speech marks. However, you must be sure that you know the difference between direct and indirect speech and how to 'report' on direct speech.

In general, the rule is that all reported speech is given in the past tense. You are reporting on something someone has already said in the past, so the past tense is the appropriate tense. In indirect or reported speech as well, you have to identify the speaker.

Consider this piece of direct speech:

'I must have maximum effort from every player,' stressed the manager.

Now, if this is turned into indirect speech, it looks like this:

The manager stressed that he had to have maximum effort from every player.

There are no speech marks; the identification of the speaker comes first; the 'I' becomes 'he'; the tense is the past.

'We need to save some money,' said Dot. 'We must stop spending it.'

In reported or indirect speech, this becomes:

Dot said that they had to save some money and that they had to stop spending it.

Often in indirect speech **that** is used to join the identification of the speaker to the reported speech, as in these newspaper headlines:

Politician Said That Health Service Was in Crisis

Robber Boasted That He Was In The Money

Activity 6

Read the following account of an accident told mostly in direct speech. Rewrite the passage by turning the direct speech into reported speech.

'I was driving at around forty miles an hour,' said the motorist.
    'That's not true,' said the pedestrian. 'He was doing nearer sixty.'
    'One at a time,' said the policeman. 'You'll get your chance.'
    'I was definitely doing forty miles an hour,' repeated the motorist.
    'I remember looking at the speedometer just at the time of the accident.'
    'Why did you do that?' asked the policeman. 'Weren't you watching the road?'
    'Of course I was,' said the motorist, 'but I'm a very careful driver and I wanted to make sure I was below the speed limit.'
    'I don't believe him,' said the pedestrian.

SKILLCHECK

Check these statements to assess what you have learnt from this section. If you cannot honestly tick all of these statements, then go back over the relevant section.

❑ I understand the difference between direct and indirect speech.

❑ I have learned how to punctuate direct speech.

❑ I realise that a new paragraph has to be started each time there is a new speaker.

❑ I know how to turn direct speech into reported or indirect speech.

4
CAPITAL
LETTERS

WHEN TO USE CAPITAL LETTERS

1 Climb every mountain, ford every stream!

2 I love New York!

3 Lord Beetroot in Bermondsey

4 Easter Monday is on March 28th this year.

5 Dear Ms Reynolds,

6 The sun descending in the west,
    The evening star does shine;
The birds are silent in their nest,
    And I must seek for mine.

7 'Les Misérables' is to be filmed.

8 The local MP has gone missing.

The eight examples above illustrate some of the instances when capital letters must be used.

Example 1 begins with a capital letter (*Climb*), because that indicates the start of a sentence.

Example 2 has a capital *I*; the personal pronoun in the first person singular **always** has a capital letter. There are also capital letters in *New York* because it is the name of a city.

Example 3 has two further examples of the use of capital letters: *Lord Beetroot* is a title so capital letters are necessary for both words.

Example 4 has a capital letter for a festival (*Easter*), for a day of the week (*Monday*) and for a month (*March*).

Example 5 shows how a capital letter is used at the beginning of the greeting of a letter; note, too, the capital letter for *Ms*, which is a title.

Example 6 shows how poetry **usually** has a capital letter at the beginning of each new line. However, this is not always the case.

Example 7 has capital letters in *Les Misérables* because it is the title of a show.

Example 8 shows how the abbreviation *MP*, short for Member of Parliament, has to have capital letters.

CAPITALS AT THE BEGINNING OF SENTENCES

Understanding when a capital letter is required in the writing of sentences depends on your recognising when one sentence ends and another begins.

Read the following job advertisement. Capital letters and full stops have been left out. Read aloud and decide where one sentence ends and another begins. Decide where capital letters are required for the beginning of sentences and where full stops are needed.

HAIRDRESSERS REQUIRED

a new vacancy has become available at Hairwego for a top stylist manager/ess applicants must be experienced, reliable, of smart appearance and enthusiastic with an outgoing personality qualifications in all aspects of hairdressing are required previous managerial experience will be an advantage an excellent salary is offered for the right applicant please telephone for further details.

If you read that advertisement aloud to yourself, you should have sensed from the flow of meaning where one sentence ended and another began. The punctuated version reads like this:

A new vacancy has become available at Hairwego for a top stylist manager/ess. Applicants must be experienced, reliable, of smart appearance and enthusiastic, with an outgoing personality. Qualifications in all aspects of hairdressing are required. Previous managerial experience will be an advantage. An excellent salary is offered for the right applicant. Please telephone for further details.

Even when incomplete or minor sentences are used, in direct speech or as dialogue in a play, capital letters have to be used each time something 'new' is spoken:

HOST Coffee?

GUEST No, thank you.

HOST Tea then? Or something stronger?

GUEST Fine. A glass of wine, please.

HOST White or red? Dry or fruity?

GUEST Red. Fruity, please.

HOST Anything to eat?

GUEST Wouldn't say no. Hungry. Ages since I ate.

Nora hesitated. What could she say?
'Goodness. This is difficult. Don't know what to say. As usual, lost for words. I appreciate everything you've done. But . . . The answer's no, I'm afraid. Terribly sorry.'

CAPITAL LETTERS

4

✓ Checkpoint A

Read the following set of instructions. Capital letters at the beginning of sentences have beem omitted, as well as full stops at the end of sentences. Decide where they should be.

firstly, press the programme button select the channel you wish to record from the days of the week will flash on the panel choose the correct day for the programme you wish to record having done that, insert the starting time of the desired recording when this is completed, choose the time at which you wish recording to stop transfer the information to the video recorder by pressing the 'transfer' button the final step is to press simultaneously the record and timer buttons your video recorder should now be set to record

Activities 1,2 and 3

1 Read the following job advertisement. Capital letters and full stops have again been omitted. Rewrite the advertisement inserting capital letters and full stops where appropriate.

Homecare assistants are required for varied duties within the local community employment is available now for applicants willing to work flexible hours own transport and/or a driving licence would be an advantage please telephone for further details and appointment for interview

45

2 Read the following dialogue. Capital letters, full stops and question marks have been omitted. Rewrite the passage inserting these where appropriate.

WOMAN cold day more to come too weather forecast

MAN always wrong the weather forecast remember the big storm

WOMAN yes still, not always they're sometimes right not very often, mind you

MAN no, not very often you can say that again a bunch of clowns really

WOMAN wouldn't say that not a bunch of clowns a bit strong that

MAN do you think so I don't think so not a bit strong

WOMAN an exaggeration then a bit of an exaggeration yes

MAN not at all I never exaggerate leave that to you

WOMAN cheek I say what I think never exaggerate nonsense

MAN pull the other one no they always get it wrong a bunch of clowns really

Read the following opening to a story, which uses mainly direct speech. Capital letters, full stops, exclamation and question marks have been omitted. Rewrite the passage inserting these where appropriate.

'i tell you there's something in the east wing a presence of some sort yes, a presence don't know how else to describe it'

Tom looked at Laura doubtfully.

'Crazy you're crazy a presence what do you mean ghosts'

'something like that i can feel it no kidding, i'm serious'

'yes serious, indeed seriously mad, you mean you believe in ghosts now, do you watch too much television made you dotty'

'nonsense, Tom you only believe what your so-called intellect tells you to believe there are things beyond rational thought things we don't understand yet'

'like ghosts i suppose what else elves and gnomes creatures from outer space'

'what's that behind you no it's her the governess'

'stop fooling around i don't believe it what is it something there can't make it out'

'a ghost it's a ghost now call me dotty'

PROPER NAMES AND PLACE NAMES

When we address an envelope, we have to use capital letters for the following:

Mr Robert Reid
24 Brisbane Street
Surrenden
Blatchingham
Wiltshire
BL3 WP2A
England

Mrs Florence Brown
'Dunroamin'
62 Inverness Place
Aberdeen
AB4 2TU
Scotland

- the title of the addressee:
  Mr, Ms, Mrs, Miss, Dr etc.
- the street or name of the house
- the district or area
- the town or village
- the county
- the postcode
- the country

Sharon kelly
6 Acacia Avenue
Britley
Longshire
England
Great Britain
Europe
The World
The Universe

Place names in general take capital letters:

Fish for salmon in the silvery depths of the River Dee.
Explore the Sahara Desert on an Adventure Trail holiday!
In the heart of Africa, that mysterious continent, a man finds himself and passion. . .

Notice that when a river, mountain, desert, ocean etc. is named, both parts of the name have capital letters:

Adrift in the Atlantic Ocean, they were alone for days and days. . .
They dared Mount Everest and came back alive. . .

Look at these further uses of capital letters:

Choosy Crackers are a must with cheese!
Visit Ludlow Castle, a historic monument of great beauty.
The United Nations fails to act.
Glasgow Rangers poised to win.

Christianity and Islam must learn to understand each other, says bishop.
The Labour Party stands for the rights of the people.
The Tory Party defends the individual.
President Clinton will visit Britain in the new year.
France to go it alone.
Americans are staying at home this year.
More people are learning Japanese than ever before.
Uncle George is my favourite relative.

These examples illustrate how capital letters should be used for:

- brand names (Choosy Crackers)
- buildings (Ludlow Castle)
- organisations (United Nations)
- teams (Glasgow Rangers)
- religions or beliefs (Christianity, Islam)
- political parties (Labour Party, Tory Party)
- formal titles (President Clinton)
- countries (France)
- nationalities (Americans)
- languages (Japanese)
- relatives (Uncle George)

✓ Checkpoint B

1 Read the following extract from a travel brochure. Capital letters have been omitted. Decide where you think they are required.

A Day in thakeray, the historic medieval city

thakeray is a town drenched in history. king john raised his standard here when he was faced with a bit of local bother. sir thomas more slept in the medieval inn, the george, a few times. thakeray cathedral is among the most glorious in england. Then there is kent castle, built by lord bolchester and designed by christopher penn. Indeed, thakeray is a maze of historic sights as well as being a modern centre of importance. Organisations such as british buses, the bank of kent and animal aid have their headquarters here. So thakeray's not just a pretty face, as they say. It's a thriving modern city with its own successful soccer team, the Thakerovers. Pay us a visit.

2 Read the following letter. Capital letters have been omitted. Rewrite the letter, inserting the missing capitals.

dear jane

guess what? i have mr jones for french again! Would you believe my luck? And mrs pannett for german! The one good thing that's happened is that we're going on a trip to london next week and we're going to see downing street, buckingham palace, madame tussaud's and regent's park zoo. Hope to see 'sunset boulevard', 'cats', 'the mousetrap' or 'rockin' with the zombies

Where are you going for your holidays this year? We're thinking of going to the bahamas, well, that's where mum wants to go. However, dad wants to go to alicante, so there's hope. Better than clacton anyway. We went out for an italian meal the other night, would you believe it? I never thought dad would eat anything but roast beef, but aunt ethel persuaded him. Next he'll be eating indian or chinese takeaways, as he moves into the second half of the twentieth century.

I went to the monteith motor musem last sunday and saw lots of old jaguars, bentleys, austins and sprites. Have you tried that new ice cream they have now in the supermarkets: tom and jerry's southern flavours? Gorgeous!

Have to go now. aston villa are still near the bottom, but tranmere rovers are doing well.

love

Jackie

TITLES

When a title of an institution or organisation, a film, television programme, book or play consists of several words, it is usual to use capital letters for the **first** word and **important** words, but to leave later **small** words such as 'of', 'a', 'with', 'in' etc. in lower case letters:

University of Sussex
Department of Education and Science
'The Sound of Music'
Steptoe and Son
Days of Wine and Roses
War and Peace

Special days of the year always take capital letters:

New Year's Eve   Boxing Day   Yom Kippur   Ramadan
Mother's Day   Father's Day   Bank Holiday Monday

Days and months always need capital letters:

Tuesday, the sixth of February   Friday, 4th December

Activities 4 and 5

4 Read the following list of the week's most popular television programmes. Rewrite the list inserting capital letters where necessary.

a) coronation street (itv)

b) eastEnders (bbc)

c) the national lottery (bbc)

d) last of the mohicans (film: itv)

e) news at ten (thursday: itv)

f) blind date (itv)

g) the silence of the lambs (film: bbc)

h) england vs. germany (bbc)

i) one foot in the grave (bbc)

j) it'll be alright on the night (itv)

5 Read the following advertisement. Capital letters have been omitted. Rewrite the advert, inserting capital letters where you think they are necessary.

monumental pictures and channel six are proud to announce. . .
On boxing day the national release of the epic production

farewell to paradise

based on the best-selling novel
'the mistress of banderley" by daphne laurier and starring

clink pasteboard
beryl drip
karen sloane
dickie dorque

Set amidst the gigantic splendour of the arizona desert,
where passions erupt like mount vesuvius!
Bigger than 'ben hur', 'gone with the wind' and 'star wars'
all rolled into one epic movie!
If you only see one movie this year, make it 'farewell to paradise'.

■ ABBREVIATIONS

Very often the names of organisations are abbreviated to their initial letters. When this happens, the initials must be in capital letters:

SO JJ THE MP YOU KNOW, WENT TO THE AA, THE RAC, ICI AND BP NO LESS AND OFFERED TO HELP AND THEY TOLD HIM TO TRY THE BBC, OR WORDS TO THAT EFFECT...

- British Rail   BR
- Royal Society for the Prevention of Cruelty to Children   RSPCA
- National Council of Civil Liberties   NCCL
- United Nations   UN
- North Atlantic Treaty Organisation   NATO
- Automobile Association   AA
- Royal Automobile Club   RAC
- Independent Television Authority   ITV
- British Broadcasting Corporation   BBC

SKILLCHECK Check these statements to assess what you have learnt from this section. If you cannot honestly tick all of these statements, than go back over the relevant section.

❑ I understand that every complete sentence must begin with a capital letter.

❑ I realise that in direct speech every new utterance has to have a capital letter.

❑ In writing dialogue in a play, each separate utterance starts with a capital letter.

❑ I understand how place and proper names have to have capital letters.

❑ I know how to use capital letters in letter-writing.

❑ I realise that titles need capital letters, as do abbreviations of the names of organisations.

5

A P O S T R O P H E S

WHEN TO USE APOSTROPHES

It's a lovely today today
That's my boy!
A man's got to do what a man's got to do.
I'm singing in the rain. . .
His Master's Voice
Her Majesty's Theatre

All the above use an apostrophe: an apostrophe is a comma that is 'raised' from the line. Apostrophes are used for two main purposes:

• to show that a letter or letters have been left out of a word.
• to indicate ownership when nouns are concerned.

From the above examples *it's, that's, man's, I'm* all have an apostrophe that indicate a letter or letters have been left out, thus abbreviating two words into one:

It's – It is   That's – That is   man's – man has   I'm – I am

The other two examples use an apostrophe to indicate ownership in connection with nouns:

His Master's Voice – The Voice of His Master
Her Majesty's Theatre – The Theatre of Her Majesty

IT'S AND ITS

These two words are frequently mistaken for one another and you should do your utmost to avoid this very common error.

IT'S JUST THAT WE'RE TIRED OF BEING MISTAKEN FOR ONE ANOTHER.

- **it's** is the abbreviated form of **it is** or **it has**.
- **its** means **belonging to it**: the possessive adjective.

Ownership, as has been explained above, is usually indicated by the use of an apostrophe. *Its* is an exception.

> It's a great, big, wonderful world . . . – It is a great. . .
> Its grandeur, its excitement, its spine-tingling thrills. . .

This advertising message is about a film and *its* is the possessive adjective attached to the nouns *grandeur, excitement* and *thrills.*

In your own writing, there will be numerous occasions when you use either **it's** or **its**. If you are in any doubt about which version is correct, ask yourself whether the word you want to use is an abbreviated form of **it is** (or **it has**) or whether it is showing ownership of something. If it is the former, then use **it's**. If it is to do with ownership, use **its**.

Activity 1

Read the following conversation. Fill the blanks with either **its** or **it's** as appropriate.

> 'This is a great dog, I tell you,' said the agent. '— better than Lassie and — more intelligent than Rin-Tin-Tin.'
> 'Have you signed this dog on a contract? What about — owner?' asked the studio head.
> '— all signed and sealed. — owner is eating out of my hand,' said the agent, 'not to mention the dog. So I sign the mutt on a studio contract.'
> 'What's — salary going to be?'
> 'Listen, I can get this dog for ten tins of dog food a week. — in the bag.'
> 'Never work with animals. — always trouble,' said the studio head.
> '— owner trusts me, you understand? — contract can be worked out, don't worry about it. — going to make you a lot of money.'
> 'What is this dog? — a male pooch, I suppose, or is it a lady?'
> '— a lady. I tell you, — going to be bigger than Lassie.'

CONTRACTIONS

It's is an example of a contraction: two words joined together by an apostrophe to form one word.

In English there are many words that can be shortened like this. The apostrophe indicates that one or more letters have been missed out. Here are some common examples of contractions where the apostrophe indicates that one letter has been missed out:

I'm – I am   you're – you are   he's – he is   she's – she is   we're – we are   they're – they are

Here are some examples of common contractions where the apostrophe indicates that two letters have been missed out:

I'll – I will/shall   you'll – you will   it'll – it will   he'll – he will
she'll – she will   we'll – we will   they'll – they will   I've – I have
you've – you have   we've – we have   they've – they have   I'd – I had
you'd – you had   we'd – we had   they'd – they had

Here are examples of contractions where more than two letters have been omitted:

I'd – I would/should (I'd do that if I were you – I would do that)
you'd – you would/should (You'd say something else if she were here – You would say)
he'd – he would/should   we'd – we would/should
they'd – they would/should

An apostrophe is often used to shorten a negative with the word **not** into one word:

isn't – is not   wouldn't – would not   shouldn't – should not
aren't – are not   weren't – were not

The apostrophe is always placed where the 'o' of the 'not' would have been.
   Note that **cannot** is written either as one word or in its abbreviated form **can't**.

- **will not** in its shortened form becomes **won't**
- **shall not** in its abbreviated form becomes **shan't**

Is and **has** may be used in an abbreviated form **'s** with a noun or a pronoun:

The lady's not for turning.
A dog's for life, not just for Christmas
What's the good of that?
That's not the right answer.
How's your brother getting along?
She's been to China.
Dave's sold his car.

Activities 2 and 3

2 Read the following dialogue, then rewrite the passage replacing the underlined words with an abbreviated form that uses an apostrophe.

DORA   I <u>will not</u> be going to the wedding. <u>That is</u> for certain.

FRANK   Well, you <u>have not</u> been invited, so <u>that is</u> fine.

DORA   <u>They would</u> not dare not invite me. <u>She will</u> invite me.

FRANK   I <u>would not</u> bet on it. Your last encounter <u>was not</u> exactly friendly.

DORA   You <u>do not</u> need to remind me about that. <u>I have</u> never been so insulted in all my life.

FRANK   Then you <u>will not</u> be disappointed when <u>you are</u> not invited then.

DORA   I <u>would not</u> go if I were invited.

FRANK   <u>You are</u> not going to be.

DORA   You <u>do not</u> know that for a fact.

FRANK   <u>I will</u> take bets on it. After what <u>you have</u> said to one another. <u>You have</u> got to be joking.

DORA   <u>What is</u> the point of putting trust in friends? <u>They will</u> all turn on you in the end.

FRANK   <u>Do not</u> worry yourself about it. <u>It is</u> not worth it. <u>What is</u> a wedding worth anyway? <u>I have</u> never been to one <u>I have</u> really enjoyed.

DORA   Except ours, of course. You <u>cannot</u> say you <u>did not</u> enjoy our wedding.

FRANK   <u>That is</u> right. I <u>could not</u> say that.

3 Rewrite the following passage inserting any apostrophes that you think are missing.

'It's going to be a white Christmas this year,' said Annie.

'Hows that?' said Joe. 'You cant know that.'

'Youll see. Its in the stars. Itll be like a white blanket covering everything.'

'Whens the last time we had a white Christmas? It wont happen.'

'Oh ye of little faith,' said Annie. 'Dont you want it to be white?'

'Im a realist,' said Joe. 'Lets face facts. There hasnt been a white Christmas since Dickens was alive.'

'Thats just rubbish. Anyway, therell be one this year.'

'Youve only three days left for the snow to arrive.'

'Youre like Scrooge,' said Annie.

'And youre full of humbug,' said Joe.

APOSTROPHES TO INDICATE OWNERSHIP

An apostrophe in front of an **s** attached to a noun indicates ownership:

the man's hat   the woman's umbrella   the child's toy   the dog's bowl
the cat's fur   the lion's mane   the firm's insignia   the ship's flag

the book's dust wrapper   the film's stars   the school's janitor

An apostrophe before an **s** indicates that there is only one owner.
    If the apostrophe appears after the **s**, this indicates that there is more than one owner (plural ownership):

the teachers' staff room   the boys' coats   the builders' tools   the computers' manuals   the speakers' words   the accountants' records

Decide if there is one owner or more than one owner. If the owner is singular, then the apostrophe comes before the **s**. If the owner is plural (two or more), then the apostrophe comes after the **s**.

✓ *Checkpoint A*

Read the following report. Several nouns are used with apostrophes to indicate ownership. Make a list of these from the passage and decide whether each of them indicates singular or plural ownership.

Stores' Stocks Decrease Rapidly

The city's stores report record business over the holiday period. Customers' purses and wallets were quickly lightened as they snapped up the sales' bargains. This manager's words sum up the general response: 'Shoppers' needs seem to have been satisfactorily met by the town's shops. And the council's policy of allowing free parking has paid off. The parking attendants' co-operation has been much appreciated.'
    Parents' wish to please their children and television's power to influence what young people want have never been more apparent. Shopkeepers' ability to meet those demands has been tested, but most people have attained their heart's desire. Cashiers' tills have been kept busy ringing.

▮ SOME IRREGULAR PLURALS

Some words do not form their plurals in the regular way. They have **irregular** plurals:

woman – women   man – men   child – children   mouse – mice
foot – feet   goose – geese   tooth – teeth

When these words are used in their plural form and ownership has to be indicated, then the apostrophe should come **before** the **s** after the complete plural word:

the children's lessons   women's rights   the men's cloakroom

■ NAMES ENDING IN 'S'

With forenames or surnames ending in **s**, you can choose whether to place an apostrophe after the name, or to have an apostrophe after the final **s** of the name followed by another **s**. Either is correct:

Dickens' characters/Dickens's characters
James' idea/James's idea
Bill Sykes' dog/Bill Sykes's dog
Mrs Jones' messages/Mrs Jones's messages

However, if nouns other than proper nouns end in **s** or **ss**, then the normal use of the apostrophe to indicate ownership applies:

the dress's hem   the dresses' hems
the duchess's tiara   the duchesses' tiaras
the boss's plan   the bosses' plan

■ WORDS THAT DON'T CHANGE IN THE PLURAL

There are some words that are the same in the plural as they are in the singular:

sheep   deer   salmon   trout   cod   haddock   grouse   swine

These words indicate their ownership by having the apostrophe before the **s**:

the sheep's wool   the salmon's jump   the grouse's call

Only the context will tell a reader whether the noun is being used in the singular or plural.

■ COMPOUND WORDS

Compound words are words such as:

mother-in-law   daughter-in-law   son-in-law   commander-in-chief

Ownership is indicated by placing an apostrophe after the final word and before an **s**:

my father-in-law's house   her sister-in-law's money
the commander-in-chief's orders

When the noun is plural, the same rule applies:

my brothers-in-law's wives   my sons-in-law's demands

Activity 4

Read the following letter. Rewrite it correcting any mistaken use of apostrophes and inserting any that are missing.

Dear Jim,

My sons-in-laws' cars have been blocking my driveway for the last three days. Charles car is the biggest so he's annoyed me the most. He wears sheeps' clothing that one, but he's not very nice. The womens' gossip has been getting on my nerves too. One of my daughters has been boring me about her new house; to hear her you would believe it was a duchess palace. In-laws visits are a bit of a pain, lets face it. How do you find them? I suppose I don't pay much attention to a hosts duties, but I cant bring myself to put my sons-in-laws wishes first. Im just too selfish for that.

Lets have a game of golf as soon as we can.

Regards,

Jeff

APOSTROPHE-ITIS

In the section on commas, there was a warning about the danger of **comma-itis**. Comma-itis strikes when you start placing commas all over the place in unnecessary places.

BELIEVE ME, APOSTROPHE-ITIS IS JUST AS BAD AS COMMA-ITIS!

Apostrophe-itis is a bit like comma-itis: you start seeing the need for apostrophes when there is no such need.

For example, ordinary plurals that end in **s** do not need an apostrophe before or after the **s**, unless you are indicating ownership. Do not be tempted to add unnecessary apostrophes. They are wrong.

Another common error is to place an apostrophe before the final **s** in the possessive pronouns **yours hers theirs his ours its**.

These pronouns stand in for nouns and indicate ownership, but they never require apostrophes:

That book is hers, not ours.
This money is yours and not theirs.
Which one is his and which is mine?

Activity 5

The following play extract has been hit by a plague of **apostrophe-itis**. There are apostrophes used in ordinary plurals and in other incorrect ways. Rewrite the passage correcting these errors.

NANCY   Which books are her's, which are his'? And for that matter where are mine and where are your's?

ROBERT   There are too many books' here. I honestly don't know which are your's.

NANCY   The intelligent one's. They're mine'. But which are yours?

ROBERT   The comic's, of course. That's what you think, isn't it?

NANCY   The comics? I see. The stories' in picture's, you mean. Don't you ever read complete novel's? You know, word's that come one after another.

ROBERT   That's her's. I recognise the covers'.

NANCY   I like that writer. Good writer's are few and far between.

ROBERT   Actually, you should try picture storybook's. They're fun.

NANCY   I'll stick to my own tastes'. Let's sort these out into pile's. That Dickens is hers, that's mine, this rubbish is your's and that's his'.

ROBERT   I like movie's better than book's. And television series'.

NANCY   You and millions of other zombies'.

SKILLCHECK   Check these statements to assess what you have learnt from this section. If you cannot honestly tick all of these statements, then go back over the relevant section.

❑ I understand that apostrophes indicate missing letters or ownership.

❑ It's particularly important to know the difference between **its** and **it's**.

❑ I am aware of the danger of inserting unnecessary apostrophes in plurals or possessive pronouns.

6
QUESTIONS AND EXCLAMATIONS

QUESTION MARKS

Question marks (?) have already been mentioned in the section about the punctuation of sentences.

However, confusion can arise over whether a sentence is in the form of a **direct question** or an **indirect question**.

Consider these examples:

'What is the government going to do about it?' asked the Leader of the Opposition.

The Leader of the Opposition asked what the government was going to do about it.

The first sentence is in the form of a question and therefore requires a question mark.

The second sentence is an **indirect question**. The actual words of the Leader of the Opposition are 'reported' and therefore a direct question has not been asked, so a question mark is not required. Notice, too, that the verb *was going* is in the past tense in this indirect question.

Consider these further examples in the form of newspaper headlines:

Where Do We Go From Here?

WE ASK WHERE WE GO FROM HERE

The first headline asks a question directly and therefore requires a question mark.

The second headline asks the question indirectly and, therefore, does not require a question mark.

The conjunctions **why** and **whether** are often used in indirect questions:

She asked the chairperson whether the meeting could be cut short.
The reporter asked whether they had any intention of getting married.
She asked why conditions could not be improved.
The tenants asked why rents should be increased so steeply.

The difference between a direct and an indirect question is similar to the difference between direct and reported speech. In a direct question, as in direct speech, the actual words spoken are written down. In an indirect question, as in indirect speech, the words are reported.

Activities 1 and 2

1 Rewrite each of the following sentences by changing direct questions into indirect questions, and indirect questions into direct questions.
   a) They asked themselves whether they could afford another holiday that year.
   b) 'When are you going to buy some new players?' asked the supporter.
   c) The customer asked quietly, 'Can you take an order for some meat, please?'
   d) The pupils queried whether there was any need for more homework.
   e) The shareholders demanded to know why the dividend was so low.
   f) 'Why aren't there more women MPs in Parliament?' asked the speaker.

2 Read the following letter. Rewrite the letter, correcting any incorrect use of question marks, but leaving any correct usage intact.

Dear Sue,

In my last letter I asked you when you were coming to visit me? I can't remember whether you gave me a date or not? Could you let me know. How's everything with you. I wonder whether you've had the results of you exams yet? Am I dreading mine or am I dreading mine. I asked my parents whether they would give me anything if I passed my exams? You know what they said. They asked me whether I thought passing wasn't its own reward? Can you believe that?

Once again, can you let me know when you're coming. I need to know whether you'll be able to attend my birthday party or not? What do you think of Madonna's latest. See you soon.

Margaret

EXCLAMATION MARKS

Exclamation marks (!) have also been mentioned in the section on the punctuation of sentences. However, some more explanation is needed about when to use them.

An exclamation mark is used to indicate some degree of emotion, e.g. surprise, anger, excitement, joy:

What a dreadful surprise that was!
How wonderful to have won the National Lottery!
It's a great, big, wonderful world!

Note that the words **what** and **how** can often be used in questions as well:

What was the dreadful surprise you had?
How wonderful was it to have won the National Lottery?

In making up your mind whether to use an exclamation or question mark, especially in sentences beginning with **what** or **how**, ask yourself whether a question is being asked. If so, then you must use a question mark.

Exclamation marks are also used after interjections, those short phrases or single words that express a sudden feeling:

Goodness gracious!   Unbelievable!   Stone the crows!   Never!
Cheers!   Wow!

Brief commands are often indicated by the use of exclamation marks:

Turn it up!   Stop that immediately!   Get out of here!   Don't park there!
By the right, march!   Take that back!   Help!

In your own writing, be careful not to overdo the use of exclamation marks. If you over-use them, they lose their impact, which is to emphasise particular statements.

Activity 3

Read the advertisement on page 64. Where do you think exclamation marks are justifiable? Remember, this passage is written to advertise a movie, so it is likely that more exclamation marks than usual will be used! Some marks have been omitted. Insert question marks where they are needed.

A STAGGERING, PULSATING MOVIE EXPERIENCE

Well, your wait is over. MGM have produced the movie of the year perhaps of many a year.
What a love story. What an adventure. What a wonderful tribute to the human spirit. What a warm comedy.
How long is it since you saw a movie that merged romance, thrills, hope and laughs!
How have MGM managed this magic formula! By bringing together the best talents money can buy. Top stars. Brilliant writers. An outstanding director. A multi-million dollar budget.
Do you want to miss this great cinematic event and have your friends tell you all about it! No. Get yourself down to your local cinema.

ENCHANTMENT AWAITS YOU.

HE ONLY TALKS IN EXCLAMATION MARKS!

SKILLCHECK Check these statements to assess what you have learnt from this section. If you cannot honestly tick all of these statements, then go back over the relevant section.

❏ I can recognise the difference between a direct and indirect question.

❏ I understand that exclamation marks can be over-used, but that they are useful on occasions.

7
SEMI-COLONS AND COLONS

SEMI-COLONS

Semi-colons (;) can be used instead of full stops to separate two statements in the form of sentences that are closely related to one another:

> In Britain, we have the House of Commons and the House of Lords; in America, they have Congress and the Senate.

Two statements are made in the above, but they are very closely interlinked. Although they could each be a sentence on their own, the second statement follows on from the first. Therefore, a semi-colon is used to separate the two statements. This has the effect of indicating the close relationship between the two statements.

Notice that a capital letter is not required after the semi-colon. A full stop after *Lords* would be quite acceptable, but in that case the second statement would be treated as a separate sentence and would have to begin with a capital letter:

> In Britain, we have the House of Commons and the House of Lords. In America, they have Congress and the Senate.

Here are other examples where the use of a semi-colon is justified:

> I prefer reading; she likes dancing.
> The curtains were red; the carpet was grey.
> My wife loves walking; I hate it.
> The government were for it; the public objected.

In these examples, two contrasting statements are made, but they are closely linked, so a semi-colon is appropriate.

Sometimes, semi-colons can be used in lists when the individual items in the list consists of several words.

As was pointed out in the section on commas, the individual items in a list are usually separated by commas:

> I bought oranges, apples, bananas, pears, plums, cherries and kiwi fruit.

However, if the items in a list are more complicated, then the use of semi-colons is helpful:

The government's policy consists of the following: the lowering of direct taxation so that people have more money in their pockets; the raising of VAT and other indirect taxation; the granting of social benefits to those in need; incentives to industry to re-invest profits.

I propose that we vote to authorise the following: the building of council flats in the Docklands area; the clearing of the wasteland in the Downtown district; the salvaging of the marshes by the river; the construction, as soon as possible, of sheltered accommodation for the elderly; the funding of nurseries and play schools; the provision of grants for activity and cultural centres in the borough.

The use of semi-colons rather than commas in these examples emphasises the importance of each item on the list and helps the reader to absorb the information more easily. It also allows long items within the list to be further divided by commas, as with the phrase 'as soon as possible' in the above example.

✓ Checkpoint A

Read the following report and decide where the use of semi-colons could be justified.

> The committee has met on numerous occasions. Some of those meetings have been quite stormy. However, we have finally managed to come to an agreement.
>
> The committee proposes the following measures. Annual membership fees should be substantially increased. Every effort should be made to increase membership. Individual officers of the committee should be empowered to take steps to bring this about. Contracts should be made with clubs of a similar nature in the surrounding area.
>
> Some members will agree with these proposals. Others will not. In making these proposals, the committee acted with the best interests of members at heart. It is up to members to make the final decision. The committee makes these further proposals in this connection. Notification should be sent to each member of the proposals. Voting slips should be circulated. A date by which these slips must be returned should be decided. Tellers should be appointed to count the votes. A date for the announcement of the result of the vote should be fixed.

COLONS

A colon (:) is stronger than a semi-colon or a comma, but weaker than a full stop.

KNOW YOUR PLACE, BUDDY —
YOU'RE ONLY A SEMI, I'M A
FULLY-FLEDGED COLON.

YES, BUT NEITHER OF
YOU IS A FULL STOP.

Its most common use is in introducing lists (not separating items in a list like commas or semi-colons):

Jane Austen is the author of several novels that have become classics: 'Pride and Prejudice', 'Sense and Sensibility', 'Northanger Abbey' and 'Emma'.

Our remaining opponents for the season are all top teams: Manchester United, Liverpool, Aston Villa, Norwich, Arsenal and Newcastle United.

In both these examples, a colon follows a main clause, a statement that could stand on its own and make sense. What follows the colon is an explanation or amplification.

Here are further examples:

I nominate three authors for the prize: Smith, Jones and Brown.
The plan has three advantages: it is cheap, it is available and it is popular.

Here the 'list' that follows the initial statement is very closely linked with it. The statement 'sets it up' for the list to follow, so a colon is very appropriate.

Colons are also used frequently to introduce quotations:

He used the following quotation: 'The quality of mercy is not strained'.
She uttered the following words in the full hearing of the court: 'This defendant is innocent of all charges!'
On page 65, the following analysis can be found: 'At no time did the police endeavour to present the evidence to the defence.'

Read the following speech and decide where the use of colons and semi-colons would be justified. Rewrite the speech inserting them where appropriate.

There are three main threats to our national well-being. Poverty, unemployment and lack of social welfare. The government propose the following. The cutting of hospital services. The shutting down of lame-duck industries. A decrease in social benefits. The relief of taxation on the wealthy. Well, for them their policy has three benefits. Longer queues for jobs. More private health care. Fewer government subsidies.

However, as far as my party is concerned, we see it in quite a different light. We would propose the following. Lower taxes for the really poor. Grants for businesses that need a helping hand. Better health care. As a famous member of their party once said. 'You do not win elections by attacking the needy in society'. The present Prime Minister had this to say the other day. 'We do not believe in free lunches.' I make this reply. We believe in free lunches for those who need them. There are three good reasons for voting for us. We care. We are efficient. We deliver.

SKILLCHECK Check these statements to assess what you have learnt from this section. If you cannot honestly tick all of these statements, then go back over the relevant section.

❑ I understand the main functions of a semi-colon.

❑ I have understood when colons can be used appropriately.

8
BRACKETS, HYPHENS AND DASHES

BRACKETS

Brackets (. . .) may be used as follows:

BURT LANCASTER (1913-1994) DIES IN HOLLYWOOD

Here the information about the film star's life span is given in brackets. It is an additional piece of information to the main news item announcing his death. Therefore, it is appropriate for brackets to be used.

Queen Victoria (1837–1901) was one of the longest-reigning monarchs.

Above is a similar use of brackets.
Sometimes brackets are used to give alternative versions of weights or lengths etc.

For this recipe you need 4 ounces (114 grams) of flour.
The bookcase had a width of 2 metres (6$\frac{1}{2}$ feet).

Brackets are often used to give additional information:

Once you leave Purley Way, you are on the Brighton Road (A23).
Shrewsbury (in the county of Shropshire) is a thriving county town.
Please ring the custodian's bell (it is to the right of the door).

Brackets may be used to make a page reference or something similar:

Please consult the relevant map (page 65).
I have already dealt with this matter elsewhere in this book (chapter 3).

Brackets may also be used to indicate an afterthought or a comment that is not essential to the meaning of a sentence.

He was wearing a very unusual suit (he always shopped at the most exclusive shops), which did not impress the interview panel.
I will vote for this proposal (not that I agree with it), because it is in the interests of my party.

Brackets are useful on occasions, but it is best not to over-use them.

Activity 1

Rewrite the following sentences inserting brackets where you think they are appropriate.

a) Neufchâtel is approximately 50 kilometres 30 miles from Rouen.

b) The village of New Radnor Powys should not be confused with Old Radnor.

c) You should leave the road to the north A1 at the next junction M18.

d) Although undoubtedly she was highly intelligent all her schoolteachers testified to her great abilities, she never really fulfilled her potential.

e) Marilyn Monroe 1926–1962 is thought by many to have had a tragic life.

f) If you want further information on this subject, please consult the relevant supplement see index.

g) Please let yourself in the key is under the mat and make yourself something to eat.

h) Despite the bad weather the forecast had been gloomy the picnic was enjoyed by all.

HYPHENS

1 Son-in-law Walked Off with Money
2 Panic-stricken City Reacts to Budget
3 Three-Quarters of British People In Favour
4 Captain Co-opted to Selection Panel

THAT'S HYPHEN – HE'S ASSOCIATED WITH SOME OF THE BEST FAMILIES IN THE LAND.

Hyphens join words or syllables together:
Example 1 above shows how hyphens are used to join words together to make a compound word.

In example 2 the hyphen indicates that the word is to be read as one word.

Example 3 illustrates the use of a hyphen in fractions when words are used rather than numerical figures.

Example 4 shows how a **prefix** (co-) is used with **opted** to form the word **co-opted**.

However, it is not always obvious when words using prefixes require hyphens.

The same prefix seems to require a hyphen in some words, but not in others:

pre-school   preamble
non-stick   nonsense
co-ordinate   coincidental

Mostly, when the prefix ends with a vowel and the word begins with a vowel, a hyphen is used:

co-operate   co-author   pre-eminent

However, there are exceptions, such as **coincidental** given above.

Some prefixes such as **pro-** (meaning in favour of) and **ex-** (meaning no longer) do seem to need hyphens:

pro-French   pro-euthanasia   ex-wife   ex-Newcastle United

The prefix **re-** can substantially alter the meaning of a word if it is followed by a hyphen:

Star Striker Re-Signs!

Star Striker Resigns!

VALUABLE ANTIQUE SOFA RE-COVERED

VALUABLE ANTIQUE SOFA RECOVERED

Rewrite the following personal reference, inserting hyphens to join together or separate words or syllables where you think it is necessary.

John Reid, the ex assistant manager of our Shoreham store, is a very self confident young man. Two years ago, when he joined the group, he was a semi trained shop assistant carrying out shelffilling and checkout duties. Now he is a highly trained professional who is multi talented in his chosen career.

Mr Reid is now ready for a top level appointment. His progress in his career is a clear case of self help. His department set an all time record for the store in terms of sales. We would be very happy to renegotiate his employment, especially as his department will soon be relaunched after extensive refurbishment, but we understand his need for career advancement. Mr Reid is a very hard working young man and deserves further success.

8 DASHES

Dashes can be used singly or in pairs.

Single dashes may be used for dramatic effect as in these newspaper headlines:

We Made it – Just!

After All That – Nothing!

Dashes can be used to indicate an explanation is coming:

We have our own reasons – reasons that we may divulge at some future date.

The director has her strategy – a strategy that will be successful in time.

A single dash may also indicate a condition of some kind:

Permission is granted – subject, of course, to the usual conditions.

In direct speech, you may use a dash to indicate an unfinished or interrupted utterance:

'I must say I – '
'I don't know what to say – '

A pair of dashes may be used to indicate a group of words that provides an explanation or comment:

The entire staff – directors, office workers and engineers – were present at the launch.
The price increase – and I have already commented on that – is entirely justified.

The use of a pair of dashes carries more weight than a pair of commas or brackets. It indicates to the reader that the words between the dashes are important.

Activity 3

Read the following dialogue aloud and decide where dashes may be used appropriately. Rewrite the passage accordingly.

'The way you drive the speed, changing lanes, cornering, and general road manners they're all poor,' said the older man. 'That's my'
    'Well, you would say that, wouldn't you?' replied the teenager. 'You mention all these driving faults you don't have, of course.'
    'Bad driving and I've already explained what I mean by that is bad driving.'
    'Bad driving as strictly defined by you only,' the youngster replied.
    'After all you've done this nonsense!'
    'You blame me for it all and I know why its because you're biased against teenage drivers.'
    'That simply isn't'
    'Oh, be quiet.'

SKILLCHECK Check these statements to assess what you have learnt from this section. If you cannot honestly tick all of these statements, then go back over the relevant section.

❑ I understand when it is appropriate to use pairs of brackets.

❑ I realise that there are occasions when hyphens should be used to form compound words, after some prefixes and to indicate fractions.

❑ I understand when it is appropriate to use a single dash or pairs of dashes.

9
PARAGRAPHS

ORGANISING GROUPS OF SENTENCES

Paragraphs are used as a means of organising groups of sentences into sections within a longer piece of writing. A paragraph should usually deal with one aspect of a topic and be constructed round one key point.

Paragraphs help your readers to make sense of what you have written. With clear paragraphing, your reader should be able to follow the logic of what you have written.

Paragraphs also allow readers to have a rest every so often. If you have ever been faced with pages of unbroken print with no paragraphing, you will know how daunting that is.

Read the following letter. It has been printed as one paragraph, although it clearly requires 'breaking up' into sections. Decide where you think new paragraphs should begin.

Dear Sir/Madam,

I am writing to complain about the recent cancellation of the 10.15 Newhaven-Dieppe crossing on January 28th last. I had made a booking for a car and two passengers on this boat and was annoyed and inconvenienced when the crossing was cancelled at the last moment. Furthermore, we were only informed of the cancellation when we arrived at the port. As you had a contact telephone number, we believe we should have been phoned and told about the cancellation. As it was, we had a long unnecessary journey. Although you offered us a place on the next available ferry, this was of no use to us. Our business in Dieppe required us to be there by mid-afternoon on the 28th. A later ferry, therefore, was of no benefit to us. In the circumstances, I am asking for a complete refund of the fare. I enclose the tickets and confirmation of booking. I hope that you will acknowledge our right to compensation for the cancellation of our travel plans. I look forward to hearing from you.

Yours faithfully

L. Mayne

L. Mayne

This letter would be more 'readable' and easier to follow were it divided into paragraphs as follows:

Dear Sir/Madam,

I am writing to complain about the recent cancellation of the 10.15 Newhaven-Dieppe crossing on January 28th last. I had made a booking for a car and two passengers on this boat and was annoyed and inconvenienced when the crossing was cancelled at the last moment.

   Furthermore, we were only informed of the cancellation when we arrived at the port. As you had a contact telephone number, we believe we should have been phoned and told about the cancellation. As it was, we had a long, unnecessary journey.

   Although you offered us a place on the next available ferry, this was of no use to us. Our business in Dieppe required us to be there by mid-afternoon on the 28th. A later ferry, therefore, was of no benefit to us.

   In the circumstances, I am asking for a complete refund of the fare. I enclose the tickets and confirmation of booking. I hope that you will acknowledge our right to compensation for the cancellation of our travel plans.

   I look forward to hearing from you.

                     Yours faithfully,

                     L. Mayne

                     L. Mayne

Note how new paragraphs are indicated.
Each new paragraph must start on a new line. The first word is written about a centimetre (or a few spaces) in from the margin. This is called **indenting**.
   An analysis of the paragraph content of the letter shows this:
   paragraph one informs the addressee about the purpose of the letter and gives some essential details about the circumstances;
   paragraph two develops the complaint the writer has and gives a further example;
   paragraph three explains why a later ferry was of no use to them;
   paragraph four explains what the writer of the letter is asking for;
   the final sentence brings the letter to a close.
   Organising the content like this enables the reader to understand what the writer of the letter is communicating. Each paragraph deals with an aspect of the overall topic. In your own writing, you should aim to divide what you write into appropriate paragraphs. Deal with one key point per paragraph. Do not make your paragraphs too long or, for that matter, too short.

✓ Checkpoint A

Read the following article about the music industry. Explain why new paragraphs are started where they are.

Punk rock emerged in the seventies partly because the superfamous rock stars of the era – the Stones, The Who, Pink Floyd – were perceived by many people as being distant from their fans and living a lifestyle that cut them off from their roots. Punk rockers and their followers rejected the glamour of the mega-rock circuit, the show business aura and the new respectability won by now acceptable former rock rebels.

However, in turn, punk rock came to be absorbed by the rock establishment eager to cash in on this new impetus in the industry. Bands such as the Sex Pistols found it difficult to avoid being incorporated by the very show business they said they despised. Punk rock became almost acceptable and part of the mainstream scene.

In the nineties, the rock music industry has largely returned to the status quo. Although there are 'rebellious' fringes, the industry is mainly dominated by the large promoters who support the same old ageing stars who every so often are wheeled onto the circuit to do one more final tour. Big bucks is the name of the game and ever more will be so.

Will a new revolution ever take place in rock? Will another version of punk rock emerge to challenge the complacency of mainstream rock? Almost certainly it will. The question is whether any such force would have the staying power to remain independent of the tentacles of the corporations that run the rock industry.

Activity 1

Read the following passage and decide where paragraphs should be inserted. Explain briefly your reasons for deciding to start new paragraphs where they are.

Most cinemagoers nowadays are between the ages of 15 and 25. Of course, older people sometimes go the pictures, but for the most part contemporary cinema audiences are made up of young people. This fact has long been known by the people who make movies, especially in Hollywood. The kind of films we see on our cinema screens is largely dictated by this analysis of the typical audience. It means that Hollywood filmmakers are aiming to attract this young audience with films that will directly appeal to them. What overall effect does this have? It means a growing emphasis on special effects movies, teenage dramas, comedies and 'technological' extravaganzas. Fewer films that deal seriously with social issues or adult drama are being made. The result is that older people go to the cinema less and less. Does any of this matter? Well, it is not healthy for an industry like the movie industry to ignore a vast potential audience. In the golden era of the cinema, audiences were made up of people of all ages. If basically most producers are making films for only a proportion of the population, that cannot be healthy for the future of the industry. Most people now see films on television and video, but it would be a pity if in the long run cinema-going decreased in frequency. Seeing a movie in the cinema is a vastly superior experience to seeing it in your front room. Let's hope the movie industry can get back to making films that will appeal to all the population.

KEY/TOPIC SENTENCES AND LINKING WORDS

You should use paragraphs to help organise the material you want to write. Logical paragraphing helps you to communicate clearly to your readers.

Paragraphs are a kind of signpost to the reader: this is the way we are going so follow this direction.

Another useful form of signpost is the **key** or **topic** sentence.

The key or topic sentence is the sentence round which a paragraph is constructed.

Normally, the key or topic sentence would come at the beginning of the paragraph. It signposts to the reader what the particular paragraph is to be about:

> The cost of transfer fees for star players has rocketed. Manchester United paid seven million for Andy Cole. Everton paid four million for Duncan Ferguson whose talent remains largely unproven. Meanwhile, the financial structure of the lesser teams in the lower divisions remains shaky.

The underlined first sentence of the paragraph is the key or topic sentence. It tells us what the paragraph is to be about: the high cost of transfer fees in professional football. The second and third sentences give examples of such transfers. The fourth sentence brings the paragraph to a conclusion by making a contrast with the financial state of lesser teams.

The structure of this paragraph can be analysed in this way:

- key or topic sentence
- development of the point, perhaps with examples or illustrations
- closing sentence that sums up or makes another related point

This structure is a useful guideline on how to construct your paragraphs.

Read the next paragraph of the article which follows a similar pattern:

> The result of all this gross inflation is the ever-widening gap between the rich and poor clubs in British football. The rich clubs are aiming to be included in a European league when that is formed. This development will leave the clubs in the lower divisions marooned in the nether regions supported by diminishing numbers of fans. Inevitably the 'glamour' clubs will attract larger proportion of football spectators and more and more small clubs will go to the wall.

It is also useful to link your paragraphs together by employing linking words or phrases.

The object of this is to give continuity to your writing so that your readers can follow the 'flow' of meaning.

In the above paragraph, for example, the use of the demonstrative adjective **this** (*The result of all this gross inflation*) indicates to the reader that this key sentence is referring back to the point made in the previous paragraph. Such linking words help to provide readers with the signposts they need to see the 'direction' you are going in.

Apart from demonstrative adjectives, various types of pronouns can be used as linking words. For example, the third paragraph of the article on transfer values could begin like this:

This is not something that will ultimately benefit soccer.

PARAGRAPHS

9

The pronoun *This* clearly refers back to the previous paragraph and the point that was being discussed. It is a linking word between paragraphs.

Other words and phrases that can be used as linking devices include:

Another. . .   However,. . .   Nevertheless,. . .   Indeed,. . .
An additional. . .   In addition,. . .   Thus,. . .   Moreover,. . .
Firstly,. . .   Secondly,. . .   Furthermore. . .   The next. . .
On the contrary,. . .   Similarly,. . .   In relation to. . .
On the other hand. . .

These linking words or phrases need not always be placed at the beginning of the key sentence of a new paragraph:

There will be, however, compensations in these fundamental changes in the structure of the game.

Activity 2

The following passage has been written without paragraphing. Decide where you think new paragraphs should be started. Indicate what the key sentence of each paragraph is. In addition, link the paragraphs together by using appropriate linking words or phrases in order to give the passage more continuity.

British royalty have been having a rough time of it lately. They seem to have brought a lot of their problems on themselves, but there may be deeper issues at stake as well. The real issue is the viability of the hereditary monarchy system itself as the country enters the third millennium. Supporters of the monarchy point to its symbolic role in the life of the nation. The royal family are above politics, it is claimed, and provide a stable continuity to our ▶

government. Monarchists point to the upheavals other European states have had down through the years which Britain has largely avoided. Opponents of the system state that monarchs are outdated and represent a past that the country needs to escape. The Royal Family itself, by this reasoning, symbolises an out-moded class system that holds the country back. The declaration of a republic would signal that Britain intended to move forwards instead of forever looking back into its distant past. It is true that the Royal Family, despite recent disasters, is still thought of affectionately by a large proportion of the population. The Queen herself is widely respected for having done a very good job. The question is whether the monarchy can survive beyond her reign. Most informed observers think it will, but that radical changes will have to be made.

Activity 3

Below are some notes for an article on the subject of 'Keeping Pets'. Expand on the notes provided, dividing the piece into appropriate paragraphs.

Keeping Pets
Pets: lovable, interesting, attractive companions for humans. Owners' responsibilities: animals' welfare, health, general well-being. Animals' rights: the question of whether humans have the right to treat them as pets. Some people against pet ownership: claim this denies animals their real identity. Pets forced to be something they're not. But what would happen to animals if pet ownership declined? Pets should be treated as animals with their own identity and nature, not as toys or human substitutes.

SKILLCHECK Check these statements to assess what you have learnt from this section. If you cannot honestly tick all of these statements, then go back over the relevant section.

❏ I understand why paragraphs help to make what I want to communicate to a reader clearer and more logical.

❏ I know how to indent paragraphs.

❏ I understand what a key or topic sentence is.

❏ I understand the importance of using linking words or phrases to give continuity to what I write.

ANSWERS

Self-assessment questionnaire (page 4)

Award yourself one mark for each correction you made: these are underlined in the answers.

1 Sources close to the <u>P</u>rime <u>M</u>inister insist that he is not contemplating calling a general election<u>.</u> <u>R</u>ecent problems facing the government had increased speculation that <u>M</u>r <u>G</u>ray may decide to put his government<u>'</u>s policies to the test by calling a snap election<u>.</u> <u>J</u>ustin <u>P</u>ockitt<u>,</u> the <u>C</u>hancellor of the <u>E</u>xchequer<u>,</u> also denied yesterday that an election was imminent<u>.</u>
  <u>'</u>We have had a few setbacks<u>,</u>' admitted <u>M</u>r <u>P</u>ockitt<u>.</u> <u>'</u>The by-election results were particularly disappointing<u>,</u> but our support in the country is still solid<u>,</u> I believe<u>.</u> '<u>T</u>hat point of view was endorsed by <u>V</u>iolet <u>C</u>utter<u>,</u> the <u>H</u>ealth <u>M</u>inister<u>.</u> '<u>W</u>ho said we were going to the country<u>?</u> <u>O</u>nly a few political journalists<u>.</u> <u>I</u>t<u>'</u>s nonsense<u>.</u>'
  <u>D</u>espite the official denials<u>,</u> <u>MP</u>s are standing by in case there is a sudden announcement<u>.</u> <u>'</u>There<u>'</u>s a feeling in the air<u>,</u>' said one junior minister with a slim majority<u>.</u> <u>'</u>All the statements in the world won't quell the election fever<u>,</u>' he added<u>.</u> (61 marks in all)

2 <u>F</u>ashion shows this week in <u>P</u>aris have brought back glitz and glamour to the catwalks<u>.</u> <u>T</u>he fashion folk of the <u>F</u>rench capital thronged to the latest shows of the leading <u>P</u>arisian designers<u>,</u> including <u>J</u>ean-<u>P</u>aul <u>S</u>atie and <u>Y</u>obbo <u>S</u>treetwise<u>,</u> the <u>B</u>ritish couturier<u>.</u> <u>C</u>ritics have gone wild over <u>Y</u>obbo<u>'</u>s <u>T</u>ibetan themes<u>.</u> <u>T</u>he twenty-one-year-old genius of the frock world said he<u>'</u>d always been a fan of <u>T</u>ibet and had wanted to incorporate Tibetan styles into one of his collections<u>.</u> <u>A</u>sked why he no longer worked in <u>B</u>ritain<u>,</u> Streetwise claimed he had never really been appreciated in his own country<u>.</u> <u>'</u>I had to come to <u>F</u>rance to flower and mature<u>,</u>' Yobbo stated<u>,</u> as he was surrounded by hundreds of adoring fans<u>.</u> <u>'</u>I think it<u>'</u>s rather sad<u>,</u> don<u>'</u>t you<u>?</u>' The cheapest <u>Y</u>obbo creation will set his fans back two thousand pounds<u>.</u> <u>'</u>That<u>'</u>s not bad going for a kid from Bermondsey<u>,</u>'crowed <u>S</u>treetwise at the end of a hectic day<u>'</u>s selling<u>.</u> <u>'</u>Still<u>,</u> my frocks are worth every penny<u>,</u>' he added modestly<u>.</u> (63 marks in all)

3 <u>'</u>But where is the money going to come from<u>?</u>' Jan asked<u>.</u> <u>'</u>You<u>'</u>re full of great plans<u>,</u> but what can we do to make it happen<u>?</u>'
  (<u>New paragraph</u>) <u>'</u>I have a scheme<u>,</u>' Rod answered<u>.</u> <u>'</u>A scheme that can<u>'</u>t fail<u>.</u>'
  (<u>New paragraph</u>) <u>'</u>You and your schemes<u>!</u>' Jan exclaimed<u>.</u> <u>'</u>I'm tired of your schemes<u>.</u> <u>T</u>hey inevitably fail<u>,</u> as sure as <u>G</u>od made little apples<u>.</u>'
  (<u>New paragraph</u>) <u>'</u>You<u>'</u>re wrong this time<u>,</u>' said Rod<u>.</u> <u>'</u>You<u>'</u>re very wrong<u>.</u>'
  (<u>New paragraph</u>) <u>'</u>So what is this great scheme<u>,</u> then<u>?</u>'
  (<u>New paragraph</u>) <u>'</u>We<u>'</u>re going to carry out a sting<u>,</u>' retorted <u>R</u>od<u>.</u>

(New paragraph) 'A sting! What are you talking about?'

(New paragraph) 'You know what a sting is,' said Rod. 'Even you know it's an elaborate fiddle, a con, a trick, a wheeze.'

(New paragraph) 'And illegal,' said Jan.

(New paragraph) 'Of course, it's illegal. All stings are illegal, but we'll only be stealing money from people who deserve to lose it.'

(New paragraph) 'I see.' said Jan. 'So that makes it all right, I suppose. As long as these people we're stealing from are not very nice, that excuses the crime.'

(New paragraph) 'Yes,' said Rod.

(New paragraph) 'That's just nonsense,' Jan replied. 'Just an excuse for being a criminal.'

(New paragraph) 'Wait till you hear about my plan.'

(New paragraph) 'I don't want to hear about it.'

(New paragraph) 'It's very clever.'

(New paragraph) 'I told you I don't want to hear about it.'

(New paragraph) 'It'll be fun too.'

(New paragraph) 'Fun! It won't be fun being in jail.'

(New paragraph) 'We won't go to jail because this sting is perfect. No one will ever trace it to us.'

(New paragraph) 'Famous last words,' said Jan. 'Count me out.'

(New paragraph) 'You'll change your mind once I explain it to you.'

(New paragraph) 'No, I won't.'

(New paragraph) 'Yes, you will.' (220 marks in all)

Sentences

Activities 1 and 2 (page 8)

1 Even in Britain, summers can be very hot. That's when ice-cream comes into its own. We don't mean just any old ice-cream. There are plenty of those around.

So what ice-cream do we mean? There's only one real ice-cream that will satisfy the ice-cream connoisseur.

That's a SLIVER, the ice-cream bar of your fantasies. It's coated with chocolate and filled with nuts. The flavour is fabulous! What other ice-cream can match it? There's no other ice-cream within light years of SLIVER. It's the ice-cream of the present and the future. Don't take our word for it. After all, why should you? We're trying to sell you something: the best ice-cream in the world.

2 For many people, money is a real problem. I don't mean not having enough of it, which clearly is a problem for lots of people, but money as an issue. People get very confused and guilty about money. Why should this be so? It has to be faced that money is a fact of life.

Many people say money is the root of all evil. What a cop-out that is! Money is as good or as bad as the use you put it to. Why should money be seen as necessarily evil? Why should the pursuit of money be seen as necessarily bad? Yet often it is portrayed like that in books and films.

What hypocrisy that is!

Most people want to be wealthy. At the very least, most people want to have more money than they have at present. What is so wrong about that? It's a natural human instinct. Money can't buy happiness, but there are plenty of things it can buy. Believe me, I've been rich and I've been poor. Rich is better.

Checkpoint A (page 10)

I have been called away suddenly for an interview. It's very exciting, isn't it? I know you'll wish me luck. It does mean I won't be back in time to go to the theatre tonight. The interview is in Nottingham and the earliest I'll be back in town is eight o'clock. Could I ask you to pick me up at the station? That would be very nice of you, if you could. We'd save on taxi fares as well. Why don't we eat together when I get back? Better still, we could get a take-away, our favourite Indian dishes, and that'll make up for not going to the theatre. Well, wish me luck. I'll certainly need it. I don't suppose I have any real chance of getting the job, but you never know! One thing for sure, I'll be giving it my best shot. See you this evening.

Activities 3 and 4 (page 11)

3 Dear Sir

It has come to our attention that your current account was overdrawn last month by £25.40. As you know, facilities exist for current account holders to have arranged overdrafts. Our records show that you have not requested this facility.

As is laid down in our conditions, a charge is levied on each transaction carried out during the period of an overdraft that has not been arranged. We regret to inform you that a sum of £20 will be charged on November the 20th next to your current account to pay for the maintenance of the overdraft and for transactions since the overdraft occurred.

If you wish to discuss this matter, please telephone the manager of the branch. We would remind you, however, that it would be best to avoid this situation in the future by arranging prior overdraft facilities.

4 You wouldn't believe how long I had to wait for a bus this afternoon! There I was in the High Street in the pouring rain. You know that shop that sells videos and things like that? Well, I was at the stop outside there. It was pouring down and I didn't have an umbrella. I couldn't shelter in the shop doorway because there was a big queue for the bus. They're few and far between at the best of times and if you don't get on one, you have to wait ages, simply ages. Eventually, the right bus comes along. Would you believe it? Two people got off and the conductor wouldn't allow anyone else on. He said it was too crowded as it was. I gave him a piece of my mind, I can tell you! He wouldn't listen, though. He just drove off leaving this long queue standing in the rain. Do you know how long it took for the next bus to come along? It was half-an-hour and then three came along at the same time. It's always the way, isn't it? You wait hours for a bus and then three came along at the same time. It shouldn't be allowed.

Activities 5 and 6 (page 13)

5 INTERVIEWER But what is your attitude to this policy? Are you in agreement with it?

POLITICIAN Of course.

INTERVIEWER Would you agree that some of your speeches seem to suggest you have some doubts?

POLITICIAN Not at all. Are you suggesting otherwise?

INTERVIEWER Yes.

POLITICIAN Because it is your job to do so.

INTERVIEWER Are you thinking of resigning from the government?

POLITICIAN Certainly not.

INTERVIEWER Despite all the rumours?

POLITICIAN Absolutely not.

6 Have typed letters as requested. Have some queries. Have underlined relevant sections. Will be in office at 11 tomorrow. Loads of enquiries from advert. Seems to have paid off. Looking forward to dealing with all the letters I'll have to type. Hope your meeting went well.

Checkpoint B (page 16)

Dear Sir/Madam,

    I am writing to enquire whether you have any vacancies at present in your firm. I am sixteen years of age and have just left school.

    I have several passes at GCSE level including a 'B' grade in English and Maths. My final school report is also excellent. I can also supply references from my former headmistress and past employers.

    Is there any chance of my being able to make an appointment to come and see you to discuss employment prospects? I live very close to your firm, so travelling to and from work would not be a problem. My family have had a past connection with your firm. I would very much like to work for Druid Engineering. I hope that this enquiry is of some interest to you. I look forward to hearing from you.

Yours faithfully,
Lucy Cooper

Commas

Checkpoint A (page 20)
'Star Trek', both the old series and the 'new generation' adventures, is my favourite television series. I love the characters, the plots, the sets and everything about the series. Captain Kirk, Mr Spock, Scottie and a host of other characters have become like real people to me, despite the fact that I know they are only imaginary and have never lived. Of course, I am not alone in enjoying this fantasy, because there are 'Trekkies' all over the world.

Indeed, the fans of the series are avid collectors of everything to do with the programme. Serious collectors will buy anything to do with the series: annuals, autographs of the stars, props, publicity material. 'Star Trek' represents for me, and for many other people, I guess, an alternative reality, a way of escaping into the unknown, which is harmless and enjoyable. The episodes often have a serious point, however. They are not very violent and usually have some kind of moral message to them. I watch them for the weird effects and the unlikely adventures in space. The aliens they encounter, as they boldly go where no man has gone before, are also always fascinating. It is a great show.

Activity 1 (page 21)
Version 1: Sherry, my cat has just had kittens. Would you like one of them? Janet, my mate, at the office has said she'll have one, but if you hurry, you can still have the pick of the litter. Immediately you see her, choose. They'll go fast. Sherry, my favourite animal must be rewarded for her efforts. It's only the best for her from now on.
Version 2: Sherry, my cat, has just had kittens. Would you like one of them? Janet, my mate at the office, has said she'll have one, but if you hurry, you can still have the pick of the litter. Immediately you see her, choose. They'll go fast. Sherry, my favourite animal, must be rewarded for her efforts. It's only the best for her from now on.

Activity 2 (page 22)
Eagles Win, But It's Hard Work!
The Eagles struggled to record a 1–0 victory over a weak home team today, although they dominated for much of the game. The 12,000 crowd were treated to a determined effort from both teams, but there was little to lighten the wintry gloom. When the Eagles went into the lead after twelve minutes, home supporters probably expected an avalanche of goals, as the Beavers have one of the worst defensive records in the league. However, it was not to be and the Eagles had to be content with the narrowest of victories.

The approach play of the home team was a delight to watch, but the killer instinct was sadly lacking in the end. Although the manager made two late substitutions, it made no difference to the striking power and two late chances for the Beavers even put the result in doubt. The victory is very welcome, as the Eagles keep up their late challenge to head the league.

Checkpoint B (page 23)

1 defining: only the travellers who had been delayed, and not the other travellers, were dealt with first.

2 non-defining: additional information about the gamblers.

3 defining: only the dogs that had been in quarantine, and not the cats, looked despondent.

4 defining: only the mothers who accompanied their children were allowed in free.

5 non-defining: additional information about their mothers.

6 defining: only those critics who hated the film praised its technical virtuosity.

Activity 3 (page 24)

Student numbers, having reached a peak during last year, substantially decreased this year. Whilst anticipating a small decrease in student enrolment, the college administration are disappointed with the size of the decrease.

Having decided to offer even more vocational courses this year, the director of education expected these to attract substantial numbers. Making the judgement that vocational courses were what students wanted, he authorised expenditure on several new subject areas.

Having failed to meet the targets for student numbers this year, staff have been asked to redouble their efforts in the next few months. Considering the economic situation of the college, it is more important than ever for administration staff to cooperate with teachers to produce more students for courses next year.

Activity 4 (page 26)

Nursery nurses require patience, understanding, stamina, skills and an innate love of children. Trainees will be assessed on their practical skills, knowledge of child psychology, ability to work with other people and their commitment to the job. Qualifications in English, social studies, psychology and nursing are required. Successful trainees can look forward to a career that offers job satisfaction, secure employment prospects, opportunities for promotion and a good salary.

Activity 5 (page 27)

Purple Flood, the oldest rockers in the business, wowed, mesmerised, excited and startled their loyal audience at Ibrox last night. The Flood were greeted rapturously, deliriously and, I have to say, hysterically by thousands of Glaswegians in the huge, awe-inspiring, modern stadium.

The fans cheered, stamped their feet, yelled their heads off, swayed in unison and generally did a fair imitation of your average rock concert audience. The ancient Flood, now all in their sixties, were distant, cool, regal and unaffected, as befits rock stars of their stature. Methodically, painstakingly and seemingly endlessly, the group played their way through their list of greatest hits, such as 'One More Million in the Bank', 'The Garden Wall', 'Leave the Drugs Alone' and 'Geriatric Rock'. Roger Dodger, the sixty-five-year-old lead singer, wore a bright cerise leather outfit, which most fans pronounced glamorous, sexy and unique.

Activity 6 (page 29)

JIM   Hey, give me a break!

JOAN No, why should I?

JIM   Indeed, why should you? We're only old friends, that's all.

JOAN Really, you could have fooled me.

JIM   Of course, you won't tell me what I'm supposed to have done.

JOAN No, naturally, I won't.

JIM   Great, thanks very much.

JOAN Oh, don't be so sarcastic.

JIM   Well, what do you expect? Understanding?

JOAN As a matter of fact, yes, I do.

Activity 7 (page 31)

65 Charnel Lane,
Middleton, MT1 2RF

15 February, 1988

Dear Dorothy,

    I thought I had to write to you to tell you of my surprise, joy and excitement about the GCSE exams. Yes, I mean how many good grades I managed.

    Maths, biology, French, English, history, science and social studies were my successes and only in geography, German and drama was I really disappointed. Well, I was really excited when I received those results, I can tell you.

    Naturally, I'm very interested to hear how you got on. Please write to me as soon as possible with your news. I hope, of course, that you've done as well as I have.

        Love,

           Karen

Punctuating speech

Checkpoint A (page 33)

1 Indirect   **2** Indirect   **3** Direct   **4** Direct   **5** Indirect   **6** Direct

Activity 1 (page 34)

a) "Was it John Donne who wrote, 'No man is an island'?" she asked. (Or start with single commas and then use double. This alternative applies throughout.)

b) 'I can't remember the name of the movie. Maybe it was "Plan Nine From Outer Space" or "Brain From Mars". Anyway, it was decidedly the worst movie I've ever seen. And that includes "The Sound of Music",' he added.

c) "On the syllabus this term are 'Of Mice and Men', 'Sons and Lovers', 'Great Expectations' and 'On the Black Hill'," said the teacher.

d) 'Can I quote you what the Prime Minister actually said? She said, "Where there was war, let there be peace." That's what she said.'

e) 'Let's go and see that movie. What's it called? "Exterminator 27." Let me quote you what the newspaper critic said. "A must for all action fans, a mind-blowing cinematic experience." There you are. Let's go.'

Activity 2 (page 36)
Duke donned his special telescopic glasses.
    'There's something moving out there,' he said. 'I can't quite make it out yet. It must be about two thousand miles away.'
    Louie made a restless sound.
    'Patience, Louie,' Duke said, 'you'll get your chance for action.'
    'Droongg?' howled Louie.
    'How do I know?' Duke retorted. 'You daft Dookie! I'm not psychic.'
    'Calling Duke Stargoer! Calling Duke Stargoer!' Someone was calling him on his interplanetary mobile.
    'Yeh? This is Stargoer. Who's calling? Over.'
    'Who do you think's calling, you chump? This is Fran Solitaire.'
    'Solitaire! Have they got you back in harness?' replied Duke.
    'For a price,' said Solitaire, 'only for a high price.'
    'Same old Fran,' replied Duke. 'You never do anything for nothing.'

Checkpoint B (page 37)
1 Not interrupted   **2** Interrupted   **3** Interrupted   **4** Not interrupted

Activity 3 (page 38)
    'Take a seat,' Farlowe said. 'I didn't catch the name.'
    'I didn't throw it,' the woman said. 'You may call me Mrs Amstrad.'
    'May I indeed?' said Farlowe in his most biting tone. 'That's just grand.'
    'Am I speaking to Mr Dick Farlowe, private detective?' the woman asked.
    'If you're not, you've come to the wrong office,' Farlowe replied, 'and I don't know who I am.'
    'Does anyone of us know who we are?' replied the visitor.
    'Ah, a philosopher!' said Farlowe. 'I've always wanted to meet one.'
    'Well, now you have,' said the woman. 'I have a job for you, Mr Farlowe.'
    'Times are bad,' said Farlowe, 'and I could use the business.'
    'Never advertise yourself as unsuccessful, Mr Farlowe,' Mrs Amstrad said. 'It's not good for your business which isn't good in the first place. No one wants to employ a failure.'
    'I can see you're not only a philosopher but a psychologist as well,' Farlowe said coolly. 'Have you any other talents?'
    'None that would interest you,' she replied.
    'Try me,' said Farlowe. 'You might surprise yourself and me.'

Activities 4 and 5 (page 40)

4   'So when did you stumble across the body?' asked Leila Brogan.

'Who wants to know?' replied the old man.

'Oh, sorry, my name is Leila Brogan. I'm a detective.'

'You're a what?' asked the old man incredulously.

'A detective,' said Leila. 'Of the private kind.'

'Like in them books?'

'Yes, like in them books,' replied Leila. 'Now at what time did you discover the dead body?'

'I can't remember. Anyway, I've told all this to the police who came.'

'Well, tell me again.'

'Why should I?' said the old man. 'You're not the police.'

'No, I'm not,' replied Leila patiently, 'but I've been asked by the family to look into this murder.'

'Murder! Who said it was murder?' the old man erupted.

'All right, then, a death in mysterious circumstances. Now what time did you come across this body that died in these mysterious circumstances?'

'I don't need to talk to you,' said the old man. 'You can't force me to.'

'That's true,' sighed Leila, 'but I just thought you might want to help and to clear yourself of any suspicion.'

'What do you mean by that?' exploded the old man.

5   'Tell me, Mr Vincent,' said Lady Hawke haughtily, 'where do your family come from?'

'Shropshire,' said Vincent.

'Indeed!' said Lady Hawke. 'I don't recall any Vincents from Shropshire.'

'Really, Mummy, don't be such a snob,' interjected Emily. 'I'm sure there's nothing wrong with his family.'

'One must be so careful these days,' said Lady Hawke.

'I say, steady on, old gal,' intervened Lord Hawke. 'Twentieth-century and all that, you know.'

'I simply want to marry your daughter,' said Vincent.

'Simply!' exclaimed Lady Hawke. 'Simply, he says!'

'And I want to marry him,' said Emily.

'We'll see about that,' shouted Lady Hawke.

'Yes, we shall,' said Emily.

'Let's not have a row,' said Lord Hawke.

'Why not?' said Emily. 'It's about time we had a jolly good row in this family.'

'I don't want to cause any dissension,' said Vincent.

'Well, it seems you have, doesn't it?' said Lady Hawke.

'I love your daughter, Lady Hawke, that's the end of the story.'

'Oh, no, it isn't, not by a long chalk,' exploded Lady Hawke. 'I'll have your family investigated.'

'Really, Mummy, this is just too much,' said Emily.

'Yes, my dear, steady on,' said his lordship. 'There is a limit, you know.'

'Not for me,' said Lady Hawke. 'I will go right over the top.'

Activity 6 (page 42)

The motorist said that he had been driving at around forty miles an hour. The pedestrian said that was not true and that he had been doing nearer sixty. The policeman intervened and said only one should speak at a time and that the pedestrian would get her chance. The motorist repeated that he had definitely been doing forty miles an hour, because he remembered looking at the speedometer at the time of the accident. The policeman asked him why he had done that and whether or not he had been watching the road. The motorist emphasised that he had been, but that he was a careful driver and he had wanted to make sure he was below the speed limit. The pedestrian repeated that she did not believe him.

Capital letters

Checkpoint A (page 45)

Firstly, press the programme button. Select the channel you wish to record from. The days of the week will flash on the panel. Choose the correct day for the programme you wish to record. Having done that, insert the starting time of the desired recording. When this is completed, choose the time at which you wish recording to stop. Transfer the information to the video recorder by pressing the 'transfer' button. The final step is to press simultaneously the record and timer buttons. Your video recorder should now be set to record.

Activities 1, 2 and 3 (page 45)

1 **Homecare assistants** are required for varied duties within the local community. Employment is available now for applicants willing to work flexible hours. Own transport and/or a driving licence would be an advantage. Please telephone for further details and appointment for interview.

2 WOMAN Cold day. More to come, too. Weather forecast.

  MAN Always wrong, the weather forecast. Remember the big storm.

  WOMAN Yes. Still, not always. They're sometimes right. Not very often, mind you.

  MAN No, not very often. You can say that again. A bunch of clowns really.

  WOMAN Wouldn't say that. Not a bunch of clowns. A bit strong that.

  MAN Do you think so? I don't think so. Not a bit strong.

  WOMAN An exaggeration then. A bit of an exaggeration. Yes.

  MAN Not at all. I never exaggerate. Leave that to you.

  WOMAN Cheek! I say what I think. Never exaggerate. Nonsense.

  MAN Pull the other one. No, they always get it wrong. A bunch of clowns really.

3 'I tell you there's something in the east wing. A presence of some sort. Yes, a presence. Don't know how else to describe it.'
  Tom looked at Laura doubtfully.
  'Bonkers. You're bonkers. A presence! What do you mean? Ghosts?'

'Something like that. I can feel it. No kidding, I'm serious.'

'Yes, serious indeed. Seriously mad. You mean you believe in ghosts now, do you? Watch too much television. Made you dotty.'

'Nonsense, Tom. You only believe what your so-called intellect tells you to believe. There are things beyond rational thought. Things we don't understand yet.'

'Like ghosts, I suppose. What else? Elves and gnomes? Creatures from outer space?'

'What's that behind you? No . . . it's her! The governess.'

'Stop fooling around. I don't believe it. What is it? Something there. Can't make it out.'

'A ghost! It's a ghost! Now call me dotty.'

Checkpoint B (page 48)

1 A day in Thakeray, the historic medieval town

Thakeray is a town drenched in history. King John raised his standard here when he was faced with a bit of local bother. Sir Thomas More slept in the medieval inn, The George, a few times. Thakeray Cathedral is among the most glorious in England. Then there is Kent Castle, built by Lord Bolchester and designed by Christopher Penn. Indeed, Thakeray is a maze of historic sights as well as being a modern centre of importance. Organisations such as British Buses, the Bank of Kent and Animal Aid have their headquarters here. So Thakeray's not just a pretty face, as they say. It's a thriving modern city with its own successful soccer team, the Thakerovers. Pay us a visit.

2 Dear Jane,

Guess what? I have Mr Jones for French again! Would you believe my luck? And Mrs Pannett for German! The one good thing that's happened is that we're going on a trip to London next week and we're going to see Downing Street, Buckingham Palace, Madame Tussaud's and Regent's Park Zoo. Hope to see 'Sunset Boulevard', 'Cats', 'The Mousetrap' or 'Rockin' with the Zombies'.

Where are you going for your holidays this year? We're thinking of going to the Bahamas, well, that's where Mum wants to go. However, Dad wants to go to Alicante, so there's hope. Better than Clacton anyway. We went out for an Italian meal the other night, would you believe it? I never thought Dad would eat anything but roast beef, but Aunt Ethel persuaded him. Next he'll be eating Indian or Chinese takeaways, as he moves into the second half of the twentieth century.

I went to the Monteith Motor Museum last Sunday and saw lots of Jaguars, Bentleys, Austins and Sprites. Have you tried that new ice-cream they have now in supermarkets: Tom and Jerry's Southern Flavours? Gorgeous!

Have to go now. Aston Villa are still near the bottom, but Tranmere Rovers are doing well.

Love,
Jackie

Activities 4 and 5 (page 50)

4 a) Coronation Street (ITV) **b)** EastEnders (BBC) **c)** The National Lottery (BBC) **d)** The Last of the Mohicans (film: ITV) **e)** News at Ten (Thursday: ITV) **f)** Blind Date (ITV) **g)** The Silence of the Lambs (film: BBC) **h)** England vs. Germany (BBC) **i)** One Foot in the Grave (BBC) **j)** It'll Be Alright on the Night (ITV)

5 Monumental Pictures and Channel Six are proud to announce. . .
On Boxing Day the national release of the epic production
Farewell to Paradise
based on the best-selling novel 'The Mistress of Banderley' by Daphne Laurier and starring
Clink Pasteboard
Beryl Drip
Karen Sloane
Dickie Berk
Set amidst the gigantic splendour of the Arizona Desert, where passions erupt like Mount Vesuvius!
Bigger than 'Ben Hur', 'Gone with the Wind' and 'Star Wars' all rolled into one epic movie!
If you only see one movie this year, make it 'Farewell to Paradise'.

Apostrophes

Activity 1 (page 54)

'This is a great dog, I tell you,' said the agent. 'It's better than Lassie and it's more intelligent than Rin-Tin-Tin.'

'Have you signed this dog on a contract? What about its owner?' asked the studio head.

'It's all signed and sealed. Its owner is eating out of my hand,' said the agent, 'not to mention the dog. So I sign the mutt on a studio contract.

'What's its salary going to be?'

'Listen, I can get this dog for ten tins of dog food a week. It's in the bag.'

'Never work with animals. It's always trouble,' said the studio head.

'Its owner trusts me, you understand? It's going to make you a lot of money.'

'What is this dog? It's a male pooch, I suppose, or is it a lady?'

'It's a lady. I tell you, it's going to be bigger than Lassie.'

Activities 2 and 3 (page 56)

2 DORA   I won't be going to the wedding. That's for certain.

FRANK   Well, you haven't been invited, so that's fine.

DORA   They'd not dare not invite me. She'll invite me.

FRANK   I wouldn't bet on it. Your last encounter wasn't exactly friendly.

DORA   You don't need to remind me about that. I've never been so insulted in all my life.

FRANK   Then you won't be disappointed when you're not invited then.

DORA   I wouldn't go if I were invited.

FRANK You're not going to be.

DORA You don't know that for a fact.

FRANK I'll take bets on it. After what you've said to one another. You've got to be joking.

DORA What's the point of putting trust in friends? They'll all turn on you in the end.

FRANK Don't worry yourself about it. It's not worth it. What's a wedding worth anyway? I've never been to one I've really enjoyed.

DORA Except ours, of course. You can't say you didn't enjoy our wedding.

FRANK That's right. I couldn't say that.

3 'It's going to be a white Christmas this year,' said Annie.
'How's that?' said Joe. 'You can't know that.'
'You'll see. It's in the stars. It'll be like a white blanket covering everything.'
'When's the last time we had a white Christmas? It won't happen.'
'Oh ye of little faith,' said Annie. 'Don't you want it to be white?'
'I'm a realist,' said Joe. 'Let's face facts. There hasn't been a white Christmas since Dickens was alive.'
'That's just rubbish. Anyway, there'll be one this year.'
'You've only three days left for the snow to arrive.'
'You're like Scrooge,' said Annie.
'And you're full of humbug,' said Joe.

Checkpoint A (page 57)
Stores': plural, city's: singular, Customers': plural, sales': plural, manager's: singular, Shoppers': plural, town's: singular, council's: singular, attendants': plural, Parents': plural, television's: singular, Shopkeepers': plural, heart's: singular, Cashiers': plural.

Activity 4 (page 59)
Dear Jim,
    My sons-in-law's cars have been blocking my driveway for the last three days. Charles' car is the biggest so he's annoyed me the most. He wears sheep's clothing that one, but he's not very nice. The women's gossip has been getting on my nerves too. One of my daughters has been boring me about her new house; to hear her you would believe it was a duchess's palace. In-laws' visits are a bit of a pain, let's face it. How do you find them? I suppose I don't pay much attention to a host's duties, but I can't bring myself to put my sons-in-law's wishes first. I'm just too selfish for that.
    Let's have a game of golf as soon as we can.

                    Regards

                    Jeff

Activity 5 (page 60)

NANCY Which books are hers, which are his? And for that matter where are mine and where are yours?

ROBERT There are too many books here. I honestly don't know which are yours.

NANCY The intelligent ones. They're mine. But which are yours?

ROBERT The comics, of course. That's what you think, isn't it?

NANCY The comics? I see. The stories in pictures, you mean. Don't you ever read complete novels? You know, words that come one after another.

ROBERT That's hers. I recognise the covers.

NANCY I like that writer. Good writers are few and far between.

ROBERT Actually, you should try picture storybooks. They're fun.

NANCY I'll stick to my own tastes. Let's sort these out into piles. That Dickens is hers, that's mine, this rubbish is yours and that's his.

ROBERT I like movies better than books. And television series.

NANCY You and millions of other zombies.

Questions and exclamations

Activities 1 and 2 (page 62)

1 a) 'Can we afford another holiday this year?' they asked themselves.
   b) The supporter asked when they were going to buy some new players.
   c) The customer asked quietly whether they could take an order for some meat.
   d) 'Why do we need more homework?' the pupils queried.
   e) 'Why is the dividend so low?' demanded the shareholders.
   f) The speaker asked why there weren't more women MPs in Parliament.

2 Dear Sue,

   In my last letter I asked you when you were coming to visit me. I can't remember whether you gave me a date or not. Could you let me know? How's everything with you? I wonder whether you've had the results of your exams yet. Am I dreading mine or am I dreading mine? I asked my parents whether they would give me anything if I passed my exams. You know what they said? They asked me whether I thought passing wasn't its own reward. Can you believe that?

   Once again, can you let me know when you're coming? I need to know whether you'll be able to attend my birthday party or not. What do you think of the new album? See you soon.

   Margaret

Activity 3 (page 63)

A staggering, pulsating movie experience!
When was the last time you saw a really great movie?

Well, your wait is over. MGM have produced the movie of the year, perhaps of many a year!

What a live story! What an adventure! What a wonderful tribute to the human spirit! What a warm comedy!

How long is it since you saw a movie that merged romance, thrills, hope and laughs?

How have MGM managed this magic formula? By bringing together the best talents money can buy. Top stars! Brilliant writers! An outstanding director! A multi-million dollar budget!

Do you want to miss this great cinematic event and have your friends tell you all about it? No! Get yourself down to your local cinema.

Enchantment awaits you!

Semi-colons and colons

Checkpoint A (page 66)

The committee has met on numerous occasions; some of those meetings have been quite stormy. However, we have finally managed to come to an agreement.

The committee proposes the following measures: annual membership fees should be substantially increased; every effort should be made to increase membership; individual officers of the committee should be empowered to take steps to bring this about; contacts should be made with clubs of a similar nature in the surrounding area.

Some members will agree with these proposals; others will not. In making these proposals, the committee acted with the best interests of members at heart; it is up to members to make the final decision. The committee makes these further proposals in this connection: notification should be sent to each member of the proposals; voting slips should be circulated; a date by which these slips must be returned should be decided; tellers should be appointed to count the votes; a date for the announcement of the result of the vote should be fixed.

Activity 1 (page 68)

There are three main threats to our national well-being: poverty, unemployment and lack of social welfare. The government propose the following: the cutting of hospital services; the shutting down of lame-duck industries; a decrease in social benefits; the relief of taxation on the wealthy. Well, for them their policy has three benefits: longer queues for jobs; more private health care; fewer government subsidies.

However, as far as my party is concerned, we see it in quite a different light. We would propose the following: lower taxes for the really poor; grants for businesses that need a helping hand; better health care. As a famous member of their party once said: 'You do not win elections by attacking the needy in society.' The present Prime Minister had this to say the other day: 'We do not believe in free lunches.' I make this reply: We believe in free lunches for those who need them. There are three good reasons for voting for us: we care, we are efficient, we deliver.

Brackets, hyphens and dashes

Activity 1 (page 70)
a) Neufchâtel is approximately 50 kilometres (30 miles) from Rouen.
b) The village of New Radnor (Powys) should not be confused with Old Radnor.
c) You should leave the road to the north (A1) at the next junction (M18).
d) Although undoubtedly she was highly intelligent (all her schoolteachers testified to her great abilities), she never really fulfilled her potential.
e) Marilyn Monroe (1926–1962) is thought by many to have had a tragic life.
f) If you want further information on this subject, please consult the relevant supplement (see index).
g) Please let yourself in (the key is under the mat) and make yourself something to eat.
h) Despite the bad weather (the forecast had been gloomy) the picnic was enjoyed by all.

Activity 2 (page 72)
John Reid, the ex-assistant manager of our Shoreham store, is a very self-confident young man. Two years ago, when he joined the group, he was a semi-trained shop assistant carrying out shelf-filling and check-out duties. Now he is a highly trained professional who is multi-talented in his chosen career.

Mr Reid is now ready for a top-level appointment. His progress in his career is a clear case of self-help. His department set an all-time record for the store in terms of sales. We would be very happy to re-negotiate his employment, especially as his department will soon be re-launched after extensive refurbishment, but we understand his need for career advancement. Mr Reid is a very hard working young man and deserves further success.

Activity 3 (page 73)
'The way you drive – the speed, changing lanes, cornering and general road manners – they're all bad,' said the older man. 'That's my–'

'Well, you would say that, wouldn't you?' replied the teenager. 'You mention all these driving faults – faults you don't have, of course.'

'Bad driving – and I've already explained what I mean by that – is bad driving.'

'Bad driving – as strictly defined by you only,' the youngster replied.

'After all you've done – this nonsense!'

'You blame me for it all – and I know why – it's because you're biased against teenage drivers.'

'That simply isn't–'

'Oh, be quiet.'

Paragraphs

Checkpoint A (page 76)

The second paragraph is started because the subject has changed from why punk rock emerged to begin with to a discussion of what has happened to punk rock since. The third paragraph summarises the rock industry in the nineties and the fourth paragraph is started because it is posing a number of questions about the future of the rock industry.

Activity 1 (page 77)

Start a new paragraph at 'The kind of films we see on our cinema screens...': the first paragraph deals with the subject of what age groups mostly go to the cinema; the subject then changes to how this affects the kind of films that are made so a new paragraph is needed. Start another new paragraph at 'What overall effect...: this goes into some detail about the particular kind of films that are made to attract this younger audience. Start another paragraph at 'Does any of this matter?': puts the point of view that this is harmful to the cinema industry. Start another paragraph at 'Most people now see films...': mentions the new point that most people see films on video and ends with a hope for the future of the cinema.

Activity 2 (page 79)

(Suggested answers – key sentences are underlined.)
<u>British royalty have been having a rough time of it lately</u>. They seem to have brought a lot of their problems on themselves, but there may be deeper issues at stake as well. The real issue is the viability of the hereditary monarchy system itself as the country enters the third millennium.

  <u>Nevertheless, supporters of the monarchy point to its symbolic role in the life of the nation</u>. The royal family are above politics, it is claimed, and provide a stable continuity to our government. Monarchists point to the upheavals other European states have had down through the years which Britain has largely avoided.

  <u>Opponents of the system, however, state that monarchs are outdated and represent a past that the country needs to escape</u>. The Royal Family itself, by this reasoning, symbolises an out-moded class system that holds the country back. The declaration of a republic would signal that Britain intended to move forwards instead of forever looking back into its distant past.

  <u>It is undoubtedly true that the Royal Family, despite recent disasters, is still thought of affectionately by a large proportion of the population</u>. The Queen herself is widely respected for having done a very good job. The question is whether the monarchy can survive beyond her reign. Most informed observers think it will, but that radical changes will have to be made.

Activity 3 (page 80)

Sample passage:
Undoubtedly pets can be lovable, interesting and attractive companions for humans. However, owning pets carries with it certain responsibilities for pet owners. They have to be responsible for the welfare, health and general well-being of their pets.

However, do animals have other rights other than those? The basic question is whether humans have the right to treat animals as pets at all. Certainly some people argue against pet ownership, claiming that animals are denied their real natural identity by being kept as pets. Animals as pets become something they're not.

Yet what would happen to pets if pet ownership declined? The central issue is surely that pets should be treated as animals in their own right. They are not toys, nor substitutes for humans. Animals must be allowed to be true to their own nature.